To

MAVIS

From

AUBREY

Unto the Hills

© 2002 Billy Graham. Taken from the book Day By Day published by W Publishing Group, a division of Thomas Nelson, Inc., www.wpublishinggroup.com
Published by Garborg's®, a division of DaySpring® Cards, Inc.
Siloam Springs, Arkansas

Design by Hot Dish Advertising

ISBN 1-58061-495-7

How many times in your life have you wished you could start all over again with a clean slate, with a new life? Resolve right now to allow God to wipe your slate clean by confessing your sins and letting Him give you a brand new start.

Create in me a clean heart, O God; and renew a right spirit within me.
PSALM 51:10

January 1

As the Christian surveys the world scene, he is aware that we do not worship an absentee God. He is aware that God is in the shadows of history and that He has a plan. No matter how foreboding the future, the Christian knows the end of the story of history. We are heading toward a glorious climax.

For ever, O Lord, thy word is settled in heaven.

PSALM 119:89

December 31

Not only does Christ give directions to the Father through himself, He also gives us daily directions as to His Father's will for our lives. Determine to follow Christ and never be lost!

I am the way, and the truth, and the life;
no one comes to the Father, but by me.

JOHN 14:6 RSV

January 2

Think of a place where there will be no sin, no sorrow, no quarrels, no misunderstandings, no hurt feelings, no pain, no sickness, no death. That is heaven!

And God shall wipe away all tears from their eyes; and there shall be no more death, neither sorrow, nor crying, neither shall there be any more pain: for the former things are passed away.

REVELATION 21:4

December 30

Nothing can touch us apart from God's will. We can be sure that everything that happens is for the purpose of building us up. Remember, God will never fail you or forsake you!

For he has said, "I will never fail you nor forsake you." Hence we can confidently say, "The Lord is my helper, I will not be afraid."

HEBREWS 13:5,6 RSV

January 3

There is One who is more powerful than Satan!
This One defeated him 2,000 years ago on the cross.
Satan suffered his greatest defeat at the cross, and in the
resurrection of the Lord Jesus Christ.

*He seized the dragon, that ancient serpent, who is the devil, or Satan,
and bound him for a thousand years...[where he] will be tormented
day and night for ever and ever.*

REVELATION 20:2,10 NIV

December 29

God gave all that He had—His Son, the Lord Jesus Christ—because He valued us so highly. Since God thought this much of us, shouldn't we show that we value Him by putting Him first in all that we do—our family life, our business life, our spiritual life?

What is man, that thou art mindful of him?

PSALM 8:4

January 4

As we approach the end of the age, the head of Satan is being battered and bruised as the forces of God gain momentum. Under the command of God, Michael, the archangel, is organizing his forces for the last battle Armageddon. The last picture in the Bible is of heaven.

And there shall be no more curse: but the throne of God and of the Lamb shall be in it; and his servants shall serve him.

Revelation 22:3

December 28

Because God is a person, He feels that which we feel. After all, we are made in His image, so it is to be expected that we would be able to communicate our deepest feelings and emotions to God.

It is of the Lord's mercies that we are not consumed, because his compassions fail not. They are new every morning: great is thy faithfulness.

LAMENTATIONS 3:22,23

January 5

We Christians need to rely constantly on the Holy Spirit.
It is important that we stand aside and let Him take over
in all our choices and decisions.

I pray that out of his glorious riches he may strengthen you with power through his Spirit in your inner being, so that Christ may dwell in your hearts through faith.

EPHESIANS 3:16,17 NIV

December 27

God commands man to make choices, but only after providing him with sufficient information so that his choices will be informed ones. The choices we make have the potential for affecting our lives for better or for worse.

Choose this day whom you will serve...but as for me and my house, we will serve the Lord.

JOSHUA 24:15 RSV

January 6

Though you live to be seventy, eighty, or ninety years old, that is but a snap of the finger compared to eternity. We have only a few brief years at the most. Let's live them for the Lord.

Be thou faithful unto death, and I will give thee a crown of life.
REVELATION 2:10

December 26

Praying unlocks the doors of heaven and releases the power of God. God's answers are always right and good and best. Whether prayer changes our situation or not, one thing is certain: Prayer will change us!

Pray without ceasing. In every thing give thanks: for this is the will of God in Christ Jesus concerning you.

1 THESSALONIANS 5:17,18

January 7

On that first Christmas night in Bethlehem, "God was manifest in the flesh" (1 Timothy 3:16). This manifestation was in the person of Jesus Christ. If you want to know what God is like, then take a long look at Jesus Christ.

Wherefore God also hath highly exalted him, and given him a name which is above every name: that at the name of Jesus every knee should bow.

PHILIPPIANS 2:9,10

December 25

Are storms in your life making you afraid?
You can have peace despite the storms.
Stay close to Jesus Christ. Read God's Word. Pray.

Thou wilt keep him in perfect peace, whose mind is stayed on thee.

ISAIAH 26:3

January 8

This sequence of faith is inevitable. If we believe in what God made and what God said, we will believe in the One whom God sent.

Ye believe in God, believe also in me.

JOHN 14:1

December 24

Angels are beings who help people against evil forces. They perform certain duties, without which we could not always be able to achieve a certain goal or station in life. Angels are just one more example of how God cares for and protects us against the forces of Satan, which are constantly trying to defeat us.

The angel of the Lord encamps around those who fear him, and delivers them.

PSALM 34:7 RSV

January 9

The good tidings were that the Savior had come. The angel message was that God had come, redemption was possible, the Lord had visited His people with salvation.

And the angel said unto them, Fear not: for, behold, I bring you good tidings of great joy, which shall be to all people.

LUKE 2:10

December 23

There is no marriage that is beyond repair in the sight of God. We should first submit ourselves and then our marriage to Christ. We must humble ourselves and lay our pride and our desire to please ourselves first on His altar. Then God can restore feelings and bring healing to a marriage in trouble.

So they are no longer two, but one flesh. Therefore what God has joined together, let no one separate.

MATTHEW 19:6 NRSV

January 10

An angel announced His conception and gave Him His name. The heavenly host sang a glorious anthem at His birth. By the extraordinary star, the very heavens indicated His coming. In Himself He was the most illustrious child ever born—the holy child of Mary, the divine Son of God.

She will give birth to a son, and you are to give him the name Jesus, because he will save his people from their sins.

MATTHEW 1:21 NIV

December 22

If worry doesn't solve the problem, why worry?
Turn to God first with your problems, for only He is capable
of handling them in a way that will be in your best interest.

Don't worry about anything; instead, pray about everything;
tell God your needs and don't forget to thank him for his answers.

PHILIPPIANS 4:6 TLB

January 12

The Bible teaches that a person is more than just a body—each of us is actually a living soul! The soul demands fellowship and communion with God. It demands worship, quietness, and meditation. Nothing but God ever completely satisfies, because the soul was made for God.

Beloved, I wish above all things that thou mayest prosper and be in health, even as thy soul prospereth.

3 JOHN 2

December 20

God has erected signposts along life's road to help keep us out of trouble. They include reading His Word daily, praying "without ceasing," and determining to seek His will for our lives. Such a path is sure to see us home safely.

And when he had spent everything...he began to be in need.
LUKE 15:14 NRSV

January 13

God gives us the Spirit not only as a seal, but as a pledge. He is God's down payment, sealing our salvation. He is also God's promise to do everything He says in His Word.

Now it is God who makes both us and you stand firm in Christ. He anointed us, set his seal of ownership on us, and put his Spirit in our hearts as a deposit, guaranteeing what is to come.

2 CORINTHIANS 1:21,22 NIV

December 19

Joy cannot be pursued. It comes from within.
It is a state of being. It does not depend on circumstances
but triumphs over circumstances. It produces a gentleness
of spirit and a magnetic personality.

For the joy of the Lord is your strength.

NEHEMIAH 8:10

January 14

Satan is indeed capable of doing supernatural things—but he acts only by the permissive will of God. It is God who is all powerful. It is God who is omnipotent. We are not to be fearful, distressed, deceived, or intimidated. Rather, we are to be on our guard, calm and alert.

Lest Satan should get an advantage of us: for we are not ignorant of his devices.

2 CORINTHIANS 2:11

December 18

We know that the body is God's temple. We should not dirty it by doing things to it which can cause harm. Let us correctly judge those persons and places God's Word warns us to avoid, so that we do not get into trouble.

Know ye not that ye are the temple of God, and that the Spirit of God dwelleth in you?

1 CORINTHIANS 3:16

January 15

The dramatic story of man's lowest depths and God's highest heights can be couched in twenty-five beautiful words: "For God so loved the world, that he gave his only begotten Son, that whosoever believeth in him should not perish, but have everlasting life" (John 3:16).

This is how God showed his love among us: He sent his one and only Son into the world that we might live through him.

1 John 4:9 niv

December 17

Is your home built on a solid foundation? Today, Satan is attacking the family as never before. As always, our best defense is the Word of God. Read the Bible together as a family. Have family devotions. Pray for one another daily by name.

Put on the whole armor of God, that ye may be able to stand against the wiles of the devil.

EPHESIANS 6:11

January 16

The Holy Spirit is already in every Christian heart, and He intends to produce His fruit. Only the Holy Spirit can make possible the out-living of the in-living Christ.

Hereby we know that he abideth in us, by the Spirit which he hath given us.

1 JOHN 3:24

December 16

We should strive to live every day as if it were our last, for one day it will be! I am convinced that when a man is prepared to die, he is also prepared to live.

Man that is born of a woman is of few days.... Seeing his days are determined, the number of his months are with thee, thou hast appointed his bounds that he cannot pass.

JOB 14:1,5

January 17

Perhaps you find yourself almost crushed by the circumstances which you are now facing. Don't despair! God's grace is sufficient for you and will enable you to rise above your trials.

Who shall separate us from the love of Christ?... We are more than conquerors through him who loved us.

ROMANS 8:35,37

December 15

Like the torch held by the Statue of Liberty in the harbor,
God's light shines to signify that He is a refuge for all who
wish to flee from the storms of life, "a help in the time of storms."
Cry out to Jesus and He will answer you.

God is our refuge and strength, a very present help in trouble.
Psalm 46:1

January 18

In God's kingdom, Christ is King. When He is sovereign in men's hearts, anguish turns to peace, hatred is transformed into love, and misunderstanding into understanding.

Beloved, now are we the sons of God, and it doth not yet appear what we shall be: but we know that, when he shall appear, we shall be like him; for we shall see him as he is.

1 JOHN 3:2

December 14

For the person who has trusted Christ as Savior, death is only the beginning, not the end. What a glorious thought with which we can comfort ourselves, no matter what our circumstances. We will see Christ someday if we have put our faith in Him.

The wicked is banished in his wickedness,
but the righteous has a refuge in his death.
PROVERBS 14:32 NKJV

January 19

Worldliness is a spirit, an atmosphere, an influence, permeating the whole of life in human society, and it needs to be guarded against constantly. We must make an out-and-out stand for Christ. Our lives must make it plain whose we are and whom we serve!

Love not the world, neither the things that are in the world.

1 JOHN 2:15

December 13

Determine to put Christ at the center of your individual lives and then at the center of your marriage, and it cannot fail. Be faithful in your Bible reading and prayer time as a family and you will build a fortress around your marriage that can withstand any storm.

So ought men to love their wives as their own bodies.
He that loveth his wife loveth himself.

EPHESIANS 5:28

January 20

If we confess not only our sins but our mistakes to God, He can make out of them something for our good and for His glory.

If we confess our sins, he is faithful and just, and will forgive our sins and cleanse us from all unrighteousness.

1 John 1:9 RSV

December 12

The secret of purity is God. Seek a pure heart from God
and you will be supremely happy no matter what the
circumstances and no matter what is going on around you.

Who shall ascend the hill of the Lord?
And who shall stand in his holy place?
Those who have clean hands and pure hearts.

PSALM 24:3,4 NRSV

January 21

Where man has failed, God has succeeded. The Bible says that the blood of Christ has power to cleanse the conscience from dead works to serve the living God. This is not mere theory; it is a fact of Christian experience.

If we walk in the light, as he is in the light, we have fellowship one with another, and the blood of Jesus Christ his Son cleanseth us from all sin.

1 JOHN 1:7

December 11

Our hope is not based on circumstance. It is through our adversities that we learn to trust in Jesus. Look upon adversities as an opportunity from God to grow in your faith and to become a stronger servant of His.

And we know that all things work together for good to them that love God, to them who are the called according to his purpose.

ROMANS 8:28

January 22

Perhaps you are undergoing suffering that you cannot express, even to your dearest friend—an inward, heartrending, heartbreaking suffering. In the midst of it all, there is the promise of victory. Christ has overcome the world, and you, by faith, can overcome the world through our Lord Jesus Christ.

But rejoice that you participate in the sufferings of Christ.

1 PETER 4:13 NIV

December 10

God is able, indeed He is anxious, to deliver us from
all sorts of trouble. He wants to give us strength to overcome the
temptation to sin which separates us, His loved ones, from Him.

The Lord is my light and my salvation; whom shall I fear?

PSALM 27:1

January 23

Peace is not man's to give. It comes from Christ. Only Christ can cancel sin and create a peace treaty with God and men. Do you know this peace?

For he is our peace.

EPHESIANS 2:14

December 9

Look toward heaven, look beyond the clouds, and you will see that the sufferings that you are undergoing here are nothing compared to the glory that God has prepared for you yonder.

For I reckon that the sufferings of this present time are not worthy to be compared with the glory which shall be revealed in us.

ROMANS 8:18

January 24

The founders of the various non-Christian religions of the world have lived, died, and been buried; in some instances, it is still possible visit their graves. But Christ is alive! His resurrection is a fact! His tomb is empty—and this is a compelling and central proof of His unique divine nature as God in human flesh.

Who is gone into heaven, and is on the right hand of God.
1 PETER 3:22

December 8

As we wait upon the Lord, God may sometimes seem slow in coming to help us, but He never comes too late. His timing is always perfect. How could it not be so from a God who favors us, as we do our children, for a lifetime?

For His anger is but for a moment, His favor is for a lifetime.

PSALM 30:5 NASB

January 25

A happy life is not one filled only with sunshine, but one which uses both light and shadow to produce beauty. Persecution can become a blessing because it forms a dark backdrop for the radiance of the Christian life.

If ye suffer for righteousness' sake, happy are ye.... For it is better, if the will of God be so, that ye suffer for well-doing, than for evil-doing.

1 PETER 3:14,17

December 7

Death for the righteous is distinctively different from what it is for the unbeliever. It is not something to be feared. It is the shadowed threshold to the palace of God.

Into your hands I commit my spirit; redeem me,
O Lord, the God of truth.

PSALM 31:5 NIV

January 26

We, as Christ's followers, will frequently be treated as "peculiar people" and as strangers. We are not to let persecution distract us from our purpose—"to show forth" His praises!

But you are a chosen people, a royal priesthood, a holy nation, a people belonging to God, that you may declare the praises of him who called you out of darkness into his wonderful light.

1 PETER 2:9 NIV

December 6

According to Charles Haddon Spurgeon,
"Forgiven sin is better than accumulated wealth.
The remission of sin is infinitely to be preferred above
all the glitter and the glare of this world's prosperity."

Blessed is he whose transgression is forgiven, whose sin is covered.

PSALM 32:1

January 27

Scripture memorized can come to mind when you do not have your Bible with you—on sleepless nights, when driving a car, traveling, when having to make an instantaneous important decision. It comforts, guides, corrects, encourages—all we need is there. Memorize as much as you can.

Crave pure spiritual milk, so that by it you may grow up in your salvation.

1 PETER 2:2 NIV

December 5

God loves, but He also hates. God hates sin which is unforgiven because it sends men and women to a timeless eternity in hell. God is not willing that any should perish, but that all might come to a knowledge of Him.

God demonstrates His love toward us, in that, while we were yet sinners, Christ died for us.

ROMANS 5:8 NRSV

January 28

All things were created by Him and He sustains all creation.

*He was chosen before the creation of the world, but was revealed
in these last times for your sake. Through him you believe
in God, who raised him from the dead and glorified him,
and so your faith and hope are in God.*

1 PETER 1:20,21 NIV

December 4

God values faith, our trust in Him, above every other character quality that a Christian can develop. And how do we develop faith? By spending time in the presence of God through prayer and by applying His Word and His promises to our everyday lives.

Faith is the substance of things hoped for.

HEBREWS 11:1

January 29

The blood of Christ may seem to be a grim and repulsive subject to those who do not realize its true significance, but to those who have accepted His redemption and have been set free from the slavery of sin, the blood of Christ is precious.

You were redeemed from the empty way of life handed down to you from your forefathers...with the precious blood of Christ, a lamb without blemish or defect.

1 PETER 1:18,19 NIV

December 3

God wants us to look to Jesus, the author and finisher of our faith. He has already overcome similar trials and tribulations and will give us the power to do the same. He waits only to be asked.

Looking unto Jesus the author and finisher of our faith.

HEBREWS 12:2

January 30

Jesus Christ is going to come back in person. The Lord Jesus is coming back himself! That's how much He loves us. The plan of salvation is not only to satisfy us in this world and give us a new life here, but He has a great plan for the future—for eternity!

You also be patient. Establish your hearts, for the coming of the Lord is at hand.

JAMES 5:8 NKJV

December 2

Christ has triumphed over tragedy and He wants us to do the same. In such triumph, God is glorified. We have the power to triumph over tragedy, even in situations which might seem hopeless and unredeemable.

Now thanks be to God who always leads us in triumph in Christ.
2 CORINTHIANS 2:14 NKJV

January 31

I wonder how many of us will look back over a lifetime of wasted opportunities and ineffective witness and weep because we did not allow God to use us as He wanted. If ever we are to study the Scriptures, if ever we are to spend time in prayer, if ever we are to win souls for Christ...it must be now.

Night is coming, when no one can work.

JOHN 9:4 NIV

December 1

Christ desires to be with you in whatever crisis you may find yourself. Call upon His name. See if He will not do as He promised He would. He will not make your problems go away, but He will give you the power to deal with and overcome them.

For I can do everything God asks me to with the help of Christ who gives me the strength and power.

PHILIPPIANS 4:13 TLB

February 1

Incredible as it may seem, God wants our companionship.
He wants to have us close to Him. He wants to be a father to us,
to shield us, to protect us, to counsel us, and to guide us
in our way through life.

Come near to God and he will come near to you.

JAMES 4:8 NIV

November 30

I have heard or read literally thousands of stories of people being delivered. Could it be that these were all hallucinations or accidents or fate or luck? Or were real angels sent from God to perform certain tasks? I prefer to believe the latter.

The angel of the Lord encamps around those who fear him, and he delivers them.

PSALM 34:7 NIV

February 2

Salvation is indeed a gift of God, but there is a sense in which
we work out our own salvation with fear and trembling.
His creative action takes place through our obedient action,
and He is able to work when we work.

As the body without the spirit is dead, so faith without works is dead also.
JAMES 2:26

November 29

Before I can become wise, I must first realize that I am foolish. Before I can receive power, I must first confess that I am powerless. I must lament my sins before I can rejoice in a Savior. Mourning, in God's sequence, always comes before exultation.

The Lord is near to those who have a broken heart,
and saves such as have a contrite spirit.

PSALM 34:18 NKJV

February 3

Good works are not a means of salvation because we are saved by grace through faith. But, our good works are an evidence of salvation; and if we do all the good we can, to all the people we can, at any time we can, by any means we can, we will hear "well done" at the judgment bar of God.

What does it profit, my brethren, if a man says he has faith but has not works?

JAMES 2:14 RSV

November 28

When Jesus Christ is the source of joy, there are no words that can describe it. If the heart has been attuned to God through faith in Christ, then its overflow will be joyous optimism and good cheer.

My soul shall be joyful in the Lord: it shall rejoice in his salvation.

PSALM 35:9

February 4

There are higher levels of living to which we have never attained. There is peace, satisfaction, and joy that we have never experienced. God is trying to break through to us. The heavens are calling. God is speaking! Let man hear.

I am come that they might have life, and that they might have it more abundantly.

John 10:10

November 27

The happiness which brings enduring worth to life is not the superficial happiness that is dependent on circumstances. It is the happiness and contentment that fills the soul even in the midst of the most distressing of circumstances and the most adverse environment.

For with thee is the fountain of life: in thy light shall we see light.
PSALM 36:9

February 6

To the Christian, death is said in the Bible to be a coronation.
The Bible says we are pilgrims and strangers in a foreign land.
This world is not our home; our citizenship is in heaven.
To him who is faithful, Christ will give a crown of life.

Blessed is the man who endures trial, for when he has stood the test
he will receive the crown of life which God has promised
to those who love him.

JAMES 1:12 RSV

November 25

Two conflicting forces cannot co-exist in one human heart. When doubt reigns, faith cannot abide. Where hatred rules, love is crowded out. Where selfishness rules, there love cannot dwell. When worry is present, trust cannot crowd its way in.

Commit thy way unto the Lord; trust also in him; and he shall bring it to pass.

PSALM 37:5

February 7

Few men suffered as the apostle Paul did, yet he learned how to abound and how to be abased. He learned to live above his circumstances—even in a prison cell. You can do the same. Refuse to permit circumstances to get you down. In the midst of your difficulties, there will be a deep joy.

Consider it pure joy, my brothers, whenever you face trials of many kinds.
JAMES 1:2 NIV

November 24

"Some day," D. L. Moody said, "you will read in the papers that D. L. Moody of East Northfield is dead. Don't you believe a word of it. At that moment I shall be more alive than I am now. I shall have gone up higher, that is all— out of this old clay tenement into a house that is immortal."

Mark the perfect man, and behold the upright:
for the end of that man is peace.

PSALM 37:37

February 8

George Whitefield, the great English evangelist, said, "I am daily waiting for the coming of the Son of God." He burned out his life in proclaiming the gospel of Christ. Can we do less?

There is laid up for me a crown of righteousness, which the Lord, the righteous judge, shall give me at that day: and not to me only, but unto all them also that love his appearing.

2 TIMOTHY 4:8

November 23

Whatever the circumstances, whatever the call,
whatever the duty, whatever the price, whatever the sacrifice—
His strength will be your strength in your hour of need.

The salvation of the righteous is of the Lord:
he is their strength in the time of trouble.

PSALM 37:39

February 9

The power of death has been broken and death's fear has been removed. Without the resurrection of Christ there could be no hope for the future. The Bible promises that someday we are going to stand face to face with the resurrected Christ, and we are going to have bodies like unto His own body.

For here have we no continuing city, but we seek one to come.

HEBREWS 13:14

November 22

Effective prayer is offered in faith.
If you want to get your prayers through to God,
surrender your stubborn will to Him, and He will hear your cry.
Obedience is the master key to effective prayer.

I waited patiently for the Lord;
and he inclined unto me, and heard my cry.

PSALM 40:1

February 10

Every true believer in Christ should be encouraged and strengthened! Angels are watching; they mark our path. They superintend the events of our lives and protect the interest of the Lord God, always working to promote His plans and to bring about His highest will for us.

The angel of the Lord encampeth round about them that fear him, and delivereth them.

PSALM 34:7

November 21

The family was ordained of God before He established any other institution, even before He established the church. No one is truly a success in God's eyes if his family is a mess.

Save thy people, and bless thine inheritance.

PSALM 28:9

February 11

As a child of God, you need never suffer spiritual defeat. Your days of defeat are over. From now on, you will want to live every minute to its fullest. Every new day will be filled with opportunities to serve others.

In all these things we are more than conquerors through him who loved us.

ROMANS 8:37 NIV

November 20

If we make our sorrow and trouble an occasion for learning more of God's love and of His power to aid and bless, then it will teach us to have a firmer confidence in His providence; and as a result of this, the brightness of His love will fill our lives.

God is our refuge and strength, an ever-present help in trouble.

PSALM 46:1 NIV

February 12

Whether or not we sense and feel the presence of the Holy Spirit or one of the holy angels, by faith we are certain that God will never leave us nor forsake us.

Now faith is being sure of what we hope for and certain of what we do not see.

HEBREWS 11:1 NIV

November 19

If God had only talked about how much He loved us
and never proved it by sending Christ to meet our greatest need,
He would have been a very cruel God. But He demonstrated
His love for us by sending the most precious offering
He could make: His only and sinless Son.

How great is the love the Father has lavished on us.

1 JOHN 3:1 NIV

February 14

While there is life, there is hope. The Spirit of God is knocking faithfully at the door. If we repent, mend our ways, throw off our sins, we can yet be used of God to bring healing and help to a dying civilization.

By faith Noah, being warned by God concerning events as yet unseen, took heed and constructed an ark for the saving of his household.

HEBREWS 11:7 RSV

November 17

It is only when our sins have been washed in the blood
of Christ that we appear white as snow in the eyes of God.
No human "detergent" of good works or clean thoughts can make
us that white, that pure. Only Christ's precious blood can do that,
and it is only His blood that can continue to cleanse us from sin.

Wash me, and I shall be whiter than snow.

PSALM 51:7

February 15

The Father's house will be a happy home because there will be work to do there. Each one will be given exactly the task that suits his abilities. Perhaps God will give us new worlds to conquer. Perhaps He will send us to explore some distant planet or star, there to preach His message of everlasting love. Whatever we do, the Bible says <u>we</u> will serve <u>Him</u>.

His servants shall serve him.

REVELATION 22:3

November 16

Popularity and adulation can be far more dangerous for the Christian than persecution. Unfortunately, it is easy when all goes well to lose our sense of balance and our perspective. We must learn like Paul "how to abound" and "how to be abased."

The sacrifice acceptable to God is a broken spirit;
a broken and contrite heart, O God, thou wilt not despise.

PSALM 51:17 RSV

February 16

Some time ago two old friends were dying. The one was rich, and the other poor. The rich man was outside of Christ, and he was talking to another of his friends. "When I die," he said, "I shall have to leave my riches. When he dies, he will go to his riches."

You yourselves had [in heaven] better and lasting possessions.
HEBREWS 10:34 NIV

November 15

In the middle of our world troubles, the Christian is not to go about wringing his hands, shouting: "What shall we do?" with more nervous tension and worry than anyone else. The Christian is to trust quietly that God is working out things according to His own plan.

Cast your burden on the Lord, and he will sustain you;
he will never permit the righteous to be moved.

PSALM 55:22 RSV

February 17

Our certainty that angels right now witness how we are walking through life should mightily influence the decisions we make. God is watching, and His angels are interested spectators, too. In the heat of the battle, I have thought how wonderful it would be if we could hear the angels cheering.

We are surrounded by such a great cloud of witnesses.

HEBREWS 12:1 NIV

November 14

When Jesus Christ is with a person,
that person can endure the deepest suffering and somehow
emerge a better and stronger Christian because of it.

*You, O God, tested us; you refined us like silver. You brought us
into prison and laid burdens on our backs...we went through fire
and water, but you brought us to a place of abundance.*

PSALM 66:10-12 NIV

February 18

When you give all you know of yourself to all that you know of Him, then you can accept by faith that you are filled with the Spirit of God. That means that He can have all of you. Commitment actually is surrender—total, absolute, unconditional, irreversible surrender.

Let us draw near with a true heart in full assurance of faith.
HEBREWS 10:22

November 13

Of one thing we can be sure: angels never draw attention to themselves, but ascribe glory to God and press His message upon the hearers as a delivering and sustaining word of the highest order. Believers, look up; take courage. The angels are nearer than you think.

The chariots of God are twenty thousand, even thousands of angels: the Lord is among them, as in Sinai, in the holy place.

PSALM 68:17

February 19

For the Christian the fear (of death) is removed. He has the assurance that the sins for which he would have been judged at death have been dealt with.

We have this hope as an anchor of the soul, firm and secure.

HEBREWS 6:19 NIV

November 12

God wants the faith of man to be placed in Him and not in human armaments or physical strength. In our own lives, God wants us to be broken in spirit so that He can make us strong at the broken places.

My strength is made perfect in weakness.
2 CORINTHIANS 12:9

February 20

Do you know this peace that only Christ can give? You can know it today by repenting of your sins and receiving Christ as your Lord, Master, and Savior. And you can do it right now wherever you are, anywhere in the world.

Peace I leave with you, my peace I give unto you.

JOHN 14:27

November 11

God wants us to live victorious lives, lives that are constantly conquering sin. There is only one way to have victory over sin. That is to walk so closely with Christ that sin becomes the exception with you rather than the rule that it was before.

We are more than conquerors through him that loved us.

ROMANS 8:37

February 21

Today the world is being carried on a rushing torrent of history that is sweeping out of control. There is but one power available to redeem the course of events, and that is the power of prayer by God-fearing, Christ-believing people.

Blessed is the nation whose God is the Lord.

PSALM 33:12 NIV

November 10

We are never more fulfilled than when our longing for
God is met by His presence in our lives.

*My soul longs, yea, faints for the courts of the Lord;
my heart and flesh sing for joy to the living God.*

PSALM 84:2 RSV

February 22

Not only are we comforted in our trials, but our trials can equip us to comfort others. Our goal should be to learn all we can from what we are called upon to endure, so that we can fulfill a ministry of comfort—as Jesus did.

Because he himself suffered when he was tempted, he is able to help those who are being tempted.

Hebrews 2:18 NIV

November 9

We have not seen a revival in America since shortly after the turn of the twentieth century. But, if we are to see a revival in our nation, it must begin in the hearts of individual believers. What are you doing in your daily walk with God that will bring revival to your life?

O Lord...revive thy work in the midst of the years.

HABAKKUK 3:2

February 23

We must be aware that angels keep in close and vital contact with all that is happening on the earth. We must attest to their invisible presence and unceasing labors. Let us believe that they are here among us. We do know they delight with us over every victory in our lives.

Are they not all ministering spirits sent forth to serve, for the sake of those who are to obtain salvation?

HEBREWS 1:14 RSV

November 8

Levels of living we have never attained await us.
Peace, satisfaction, and joy we have never experienced
are available to us. God is trying to break through.
The heavens are calling and God is speaking!

I will hear what God the Lord will say;
For He will speak peace to His people, to His godly ones.

PSALM 85:8 NASB

February 24

When I see Christ hanging there, the spikes in His hands, the crown of thorns on His brow, I see the picture of God's grace toward men. I know then that man cannot work his way to heaven, and nothing can equal God's infinite love for sinful men.

That being justified by his grace, we should be made heirs according to the hope of eternal life.

TITUS 3:7

November 7

All righteousness is rooted in belief. Believe God for all His promises and He will count it unto you as righteousness. Believe on the Lord Jesus Christ, God's ultimate standard and incarnation of righteousness, and be saved.

For the Lord knoweth the way of the righteous:
but the way of the ungodly shall perish.

PSALM 1:6

February 25

One of America's best-known columnists said, "For us all, the world is disorderly and dangerous ungoverned, and apparently ungovernable." The question arises: Who will restore order? Who alone can govern the world? The only answer is Jesus Christ!

Awaiting our blessed hope, the appearing of the glory of our great God and Savior Jesus Christ.

TITUS 2:13 RSV

November 6

This is peace—to be able to sleep in the storm!
In Christ, we are relaxed and at peace in the midst of the
confusions, bewilderments, and perplexities of this life.
The storm rages, but our hearts are at rest.

Thou rulest the raging of the sea:
when the waves thereof arise, thou stillest them.

PSALM 89:9

February 26

One of the best ways to get rid of discouragement is to remember that Christ is coming again. The Bible accurately foretells the future, and it says that the consummation of all things shall be the coming again of Jesus Christ to this earth.

When Christ, who is our life, shall appear, then shall ye also appear with him in glory.

COLOSSIANS 3:4

November 5

God keeps on giving. He meets our daily physical needs. He delivers us from evil when we stay close to Him. And there is never a time when we are separated from His care and concern. How could there be? His Son died for us. Can you think of a better reason why God would care for us?

I will say of the Lord, he is my refuge and my fortress: my God; in him will I trust.

PSALM 91:2

February 27

Our valleys may be filled with foes and tears; but we can lift our eyes to the hills to see God and the angels, heaven's spectators, who support us according to God's infinite wisdom as they prepare our welcome home.

Wherefore seeing we also are compassed about with so great a cloud of witnesses...let us run with patience the race that is set before us.

HEBREWS 12:1

November 4

You should be preparing to meet Christ,
because no one knows the day or the hour when life will end
and God's angels, who have been protecting you, will then
usher you into the presence of Christ.

*The Son of Man will send out his angels, and they will weed out of his
kingdom everything that causes sin and all who do evil....Then the
righteous will shine like the sun in the kingdom of their Father.*

MATTHEW 13:41,43 NIV

February 28
2006

Fri
Feb 24' 06 Sick
in night
Sat - Tue

Shayla
wint to
heavenly home

From one end of the Bible to the other, there is the record of men who turned the tide of history by prayer; men who fervently prayed, and God answered. The problems of the world will never be settled unless our national leaders go to God in prayer.

The effective, fervent prayer of a righteous man avails much.
JAMES 5:16 NKJV

November 3

God has his own secret agents—angels.
God's angels never fail in their appointed tasks.
We will never know how many potentially fatal accidents
were avoided because God's angels protected us.

For he will give his angels charge of you to guard you in all your ways.

PSALM 91:11 RSV

February 29

A Christian's goodness is a rebuke to another's wickedness; his being right side up is a reflection upon the worldling's inverted position. So conflict is natural. And persecution is inevitable.

All that will live godly in Christ Jesus shall suffer persecution.

2 TIMOTHY 3:12

November 2

For best results in marriage and in rearing children and building a stable home, follow the instructions of the One who performed the first wedding in the Garden of Eden. Those instructions are in the Bible. You can have the right kind of home. Your home can be united if it is now divided.

All your sons will be taught by the Lord,
and great will be your children's peace.

ISAIAH 54:13 NIV

March 1

Jesus was a gentle person. Wherever true Christianity has gone, His followers have performed acts of gentleness and kindness.

And the Lord's servant must not be quarrelsome but kindly to every one, an apt teacher, forbearing, correcting his opponents with gentleness.

2 TIMOTHY 2:24,25 RSV

November 1

I have never met a person who spent time in daily prayer and in the study of God's Word and who was strong in the faith who was ever discouraged for very long. You cannot be discouraged if you are close to the One who gives all hope and plenty to be encouraged about.

Wait on the Lord: be of good courage, and he shall strengthen thine heart: wait, I say, on the Lord.

PSALM 27:14

March 2

The Spirit witnesses to us by His Word and within our hearts that Christ died for us, and by faith in Him we have become God's children. What a wonderful thing to know the Holy Spirit has been given to us as a seal—a pledge—and a witness!

Nevertheless, God's solid foundation stands firm, sealed with this inscription: "The Lord knows those who are his."

2 TIMOTHY 2:19 NIV

October 31

God thought of you even before He made the world, even before He made you. He loves you and longs to have the deepest and closest relationship possible with you.

God hath from the beginning chosen you.

2 THESSALONIANS 2:13

March 3

Life cannot lose its zest when down underneath our present discomfort is the knowledge that we are children of a King. "All things" are taken in stride; burdens become blessings in disguise; every wound, like good surgery, is for our good; and etched in every cross is the symbol of a crown.

If we suffer, we shall also reign with him.

2 TIMOTHY 2:12

October 30

We have heard the modern expression, "Don't fight it—it's bigger than both of us." Those who submit to the will of God do not fight back at life. They learn the secret of surrender, of yielding to God. He then fights for us!

I urge you, brothers, in view of God's mercy, to offer your bodies as living sacrifices, holy and pleasing to God—this is your spiritual act of worship.

ROMANS 12:1 NIV

March 4

All of our difficulties are not solved the moment we are converted to Christ, but conversion does mean that we can approach our problems with a new attitude and in a new strength.

I know whom I have believed.

2 TIMOTHY 1:12

October 29

Our days are filled with tiny golden minutes with eternity in them. Our lives are immortal. One thousand years from this day you will be more alive than you are at this moment. There is a future life with God for those who put their trust in His Son, Jesus Christ.

As for man, his days are as grass: as a flower of the field, so he flourisheth.

PSALM 103:15

March 5

Materialism has become the god of too many of us. The Bible teaches that preoccupation with material possessions is a form of idolatry. And God hates idolatry. The Bible declares, "What shall it profit a man, if he shall gain the whole world, and lose his own soul?"

For the love of money is the root of all evils; it is through this craving that some have wandered away from the faith.

1 TIMOTHY 6:10 RSV

October 28

When we as Christians die, we go straight into the presence of Christ, straight to that place, straight to that mansion in heaven to spend eternity with God. The place we are going to has an address just as the place in which we are now living has an address. It is a real place.

I go to prepare a place for you.

JOHN 14:2

March 6

The persecuted are happy because they are being processed for heaven. Persecution is to the Christian what "growing pains" are to the growing child. No pain, no development. No suffering, no glory. No struggle, no victory. No persecution, no reward!

We...suffer reproach, because we trust in the living God.
1 Timothy 4:10

October 27

If you are a believer in Christ, expect powerful angels to accompany you in your life experiences. Lord, give me the eyes to see the angels around me.

Bless the Lord, ye his angels, that excel in strength, that do his commandments, hearkening unto the voice of his word.

PSALM 103:20

March 7

Never before in history have we stood in greater need of prayer. Will we be people of prayer for such a time as this?

I will therefore that men pray every where, lifting up holy hands, without wrath and doubting.

1 TIMOTHY 2:8

October 26

This is the secret of soul-satisfaction: Let your soul delight itself in fatness. Remove the obstructions, tear down the barriers, and let your soul find the fulfillment of its deepest longings in fellowship with God.

Oh that men would praise the Lord for his goodness, and for his wonderful works to the children of men! For he satisfieth the longing soul, and filleth the hungry soul with goodness.

PSALM 107:8,9

March 8

The work of Christ is a fact, His cross is a fact, His tomb is a fact, His resurrection is a fact. You are not called upon to believe something that is not credible, but to believe in the fact of history.

For I delivered unto you first of all that which I also received, how that Christ died for our sins according to the scriptures; and that he was buried, and that he rose again the third day.

1 CORINTHIANS 15:3,4

October 25

God is sending forth His message of love,
but we must be on the right wavelength. We must be
willing to receive His message and then to obey it.

My spirit made diligent search.

PSALM 77:6

March 9

What a moment it is going to be for believers throughout all the ages, from every tribe, nation, and tongue, when they are presented in the Court of Heaven. Scripture calls it, "the marriage supper of the Lamb" (Revelation 19:9).

But when I, the Messiah, shall come in my glory, and all the angels with me, then I shall sit upon my throne of glory.

MATTHEW 25:31 TLB

October 24

The Bible is our one sure guide in an unsure world.
We should begin the day with the Book, and as the day comes
to a close let the Word speak its wisdom to our souls.

Your word is a lamp to my feet and a light for my path.
PSALM 119:105 NIV

March 10

We can look to God as our Father. We can have a personal sense of His love for us and His interest in us, for He is concerned about us as a father is concerned for his children.

May our Lord Jesus Christ himself and God our Father, who loved us and by his grace gave us eternal encouragement and good hope, encourage your hearts and strengthen you.

2 THESSALONIANS 2:16,17 NIV

October 23

The Bible has survived every scratch of human pen. It has survived the assault of skeptics, agnostics, and atheists. It has never been proved wrong by a single archaeological discovery. It remains supreme in its revelation of redemption. God still speaks to us today through that same Word, which stands forever.

Your word, O Lord, is eternal; it stands firm in the heavens.
PSALM 119:89 NIV

March 11

Whatever awaits us is encountered first by Him—like the oriental shepherd always went ahead of his sheep—therefore any attack on sheep has to deal first with the shepherd—all the tomorrows of our lives have to pass Him before they get to us!

When he brings out his own sheep, he goes before them: and the sheep follow him, for they know his voice.

JOHN 10:4 NKJV

October 22

As we look unto God instead of at ourselves and our circumstances, our perspectives change. Do not get bogged down in the circumstances of life. Look unto the hills for the guidance of Christ.

I lift up my eyes to the hills—from where will my help come?
My help comes from the Lord, who made heaven and earth.
PSALM 121:1,2 NRSV

March 12

Christ at His return will take away suffering; He says He will wipe away all tears. There will be no more backaches or headaches; cancer and heart disease will be eliminated; mental illness will be no more. All the diseases of mankind will be cured when Christ comes back.

He will wipe every tear from their eyes. There will be no more death or mourning or crying or pain.

REVELATION 21:4 NIV

Randys funeral

October 21, 2013

Only what is built on the solid foundation of Christ will last. As the poem says, "Only one life, 'twill soon be past. Only what's done for Christ shall last."

Unless the Lord builds the house, they labor in vain who build it; unless the Lord guards the city, the watchman stays awake in vain.

PSALM 127:1 NKJV

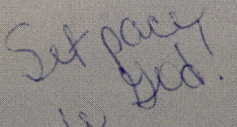
Set pace to God!

March 13

God is first of all concerned with what you are. What you do is the result of what you are.

And the very God of peace sanctify you wholly; and I pray God your whole spirit and soul and body be preserved blameless unto the coming of our Lord Jesus Christ.

1 Thessalonians 5:23

October 20

The moment I receive Jesus Christ as Savior, the Holy Spirit takes up residence in my heart. For the Christian to grow in wisdom and knowledge of the Word of God, he must be willing to study God's Word and to be a willing pupil of God's Holy Spirit.

God's love has been poured into our hearts through
the Holy Spirit which has been given to us.

ROMANS 5:5 RSV

March 14

T̲ry to have a systematic method of prayer. The devil will fight you every step of the way. There will be many interruptions, but keep at it! Don't be discouraged. Soon you will find that these periods of prayer are the greatest delight in your life. You will look forward to them with more anticipation than to anything else.

Pray without ceasing.

1 THESSALONIANS 5:17

October 19

There are eternal benefits that come from making the right choice. There are also eternal consequences for making the wrong choice. Which choices have you been making in your life?

I have set before you life and death...therefore choose life, that you and your descendants may live.

DEUTERONOMY 30:19 RSV

March 15

Readiness and watchfulness are all urged upon Christians, lest Christ's coming, taking us by surprise, should find us unprepared.

For yourselves know perfectly that the day of the Lord
so cometh as a thief in the night.
1 THESSALONIANS 5:2

October 18

Unless God is revealed to us through personal experience, we can never really know God. Most of us know about God, but that is quite different from really knowing God.

Search me, O God, and know my heart! Try me and know my thoughts! And see if there be any wicked way in me, and lead me in the way everlasting.

PSALM 139:23,24 RSV

March 16

There is one great fact which gives the Christian assurance in the face of death: the resurrection of Jesus Christ. It is the physical, bodily resurrection of Christ that gives us confidence and hope.

To them God has chosen to make known among the Gentiles the glorious riches of this mystery, which is Christ in you the hope of glory.

COLOSSIANS 1:27 NIV

October 17

Suffering teaches us patience. These words were found penned on the wall of a prison cell in Europe: "I believe in the sun even when it is not shining. I believe in love even when I don't feel it. I believe in God even when He is silent."

The Lord is nigh unto all them that call upon him,
to all that call upon him in truth.

PSALM 145:18

March 17

In an infinite way that staggers our hearts and minds, we know that Christ paid the penalty for our sins, past, present, and future. That is why He died on the cross.

For in him all the fulness of God was pleased to dwell, and through him to reconcile to himself all things, whether on earth or in heaven, making peace by the blood of his cross.

COLOSSIANS 1:19,20 RSV

October 16

Based upon what we do know about God's character, demonstrated supremely in the Cross, we can trust that God is doing what is best for our lives. As Corrie ten Boom once explained, "Picture a piece of embroidery placed between you and God, with the right side up toward God. Man sees the loose, frayed ends; but God sees the pattern."

The Lord loveth the righteous.

PSALM 146:8

March 18

God said from the cross: "I love you." He was also saying: "I can forgive you." God in Christ had a basis for forgiveness. Because Christ died, God can justify the sinner and still be just. The cross is God's great plus sign of history.

The Lord hath laid on him the iniquity of us all.

ISAIAH 53:6

October 15

God's love is unchangeable. He loves us in spite of knowing us as we really are. Were it not for the love of God, none of us would ever have a chance.

Great is our Lord, and of great power: his understanding is infinite.

PSALM 147:5

March 19

Many times we make the mistake of thinking that Christ's help is needed only for sickrooms or in times of overwhelming sorrow and suffering. This is not true. Jesus wishes to enter into every mood and every moment of our lives. I do not believe that anything happens to the obedient Christian by accident.

My God will meet all your needs according to his glorious riches in Christ Jesus.

PHILIPPIANS 4:19 NIV

October 14

A nation can rise no higher, can be no stronger, and be no better than the individuals which compose that nation! David realized this truth; and in wisdom, he concluded that he should start making things right in himself! Each one of us needs to reach that same conclusion.

Pride goeth before destruction, and a haughty spirit before a fall.
PROVERBS 16:18

March 20

The moment you come to Christ, the Spirit of God brings the life of God into you and you begin to live. There's a whole new direction to your life because the Spirit of God has given to you the very life of God, and God is an eternal God—that means you'll live as long as God lives.

I can do all things through Christ which strengtheneth me.
PHILIPPIANS 4:13

October 13

True happiness begins when one is in a right relationship with God. God is the only source of true happiness, because He offers...contentment, security, peace, and hope for the future.

But happy is the man who has the God of Jacob as his helper, whose hope is in the Lord his God.

PSALM 146:5 TLB

March 21

Anticipation of trouble makes trifles appear unduly large, and the troubles that never come make up an imagined burden that will crush the spirit. They are haunting specters, as unsubstantial as a bad dream, and we spend the strength that should be expended in constructive work and services in fighting problems that do not even exist.

Do not fret.

PSALM 37:1 NKJV

October 12

The majority of children acquire the characteristics and habits of their parents. What are they learning from us?

Train up a child in the way he should go: and when he is old, he will not depart from it.

PROVERBS 22:6

March 22

Happy is the person who has learned the secret of coming to God daily in prayer. Fifteen minutes alone with God every morning can change our outlooks and recharge our batteries.

Have no anxiety about anything, but in everything by prayer and supplication with thanksgiving let your requests be made known to God.

PHILIPPIANS 4:6 RSV

October 11

Giving to God is a guaranteed investment with a certain return. God wants us to be a channel of blessing to others. When we are, it is we who receive the greatest blessing of all.

Give, and it will be given to you. A good measure, pressed down, shaken together and running over, will be poured into your lap. For with the measure you use, it will be measured to you.

LUKE 6:38 NIV

March 23

Resentment and resignation are not the answer to the problem of suffering. And there is a step beyond mere acceptance. It is accepting with joy. The Christian life is a joyful life. The ability to rejoice in any situation is a sign of spiritual maturity.

Rejoice in the Lord always. I will say it again: Rejoice!

PHILIPPIANS 4:4 NIV

October 10

Christ cried out on the cross, "My God, my God, why hast thou forsaken me?" What a terribly frightening and horrible moment that was, as the blackness of man's sin caused the Father to turn away in disgust. Yet what a glorious moment it was, as Christ took upon His holy and sinless self all of the penalty that should have been ours because of our sinfulness.

Holy, holy, holy, is the Lord of hosts.

ISAIAH 6:3

March 24

Christians can rejoice in the midst of persecution because they have eternity's values in view. The thought of the future life with its prerogatives and joys helps to make the trials of the present seem light and transient. "...for theirs is the kingdom of heaven."

I count all things but loss for the excellency of the knowledge of Christ Jesus my Lord.

PHILIPPIANS 3:8

October 9

The Christian should never consider death a tragedy. Rather he should see it as the angels do: they realize that joy should mark the journey from time to eternity. The way to life is by the valley of death, but the road is marked with victory all the way.

I am the resurrection, and the life: he that believeth in me, though he were dead, yet shall he live.

JOHN 11:25

March 25

The cross presents itself in the midst of our dilemma as our only hope. Here is power enough to transform human nature. Here is power enough to change the world.

And being found in fashion as a man, he humbled himself, and became obedient unto death, even the death of the cross.

PHILIPPIANS 2:8

October 8

Victor Hugo said of death: "When I go down to the grave I can say, like so many others: I have finished my work, but I cannot say I have finished my life. My day's work will begin the next morning. My tomb closes in the twilight to be opened in the dawn."

He will swallow up death forever. Then the Lord God will wipe away the tears from all faces.

ISAIAH 25:8 NRSV

March 26

We Christians are not to be conformed to this world mentally. We are not even to be conformed to the world's anxieties. We are to be lights in the midst of darkness, and our lives should exemplify relaxation, peace, and joy in the midst of frustration, confusion, and despair.

Let this mind be in you, which was also in Christ Jesus.

PHILIPPIANS 2:5

October 7

God has taken the responsibility for our care and worry.
You can be positively assured that God does care for you,
and if God cares for you and has promised to carry your burdens
and cares, then nothing should distress you.

Casting all your care upon him; for he careth for you.
1 PETER 5:7

March 27

Sometimes it takes suffering to make us realize the brevity of life, and the importance of living for Christ. Often God uses suffering to accomplish things in our lives that would otherwise never be achieved.

If you should suffer for righteousness's sake, you are blessed.
1 PETER 3:14 NKJV

October 6

Jesus the Good Shepherd owns the sheep: they belong to Him. He guards the sheep: He never abandons them when danger is near. He knows them each by name and leads them out. And He lays down his life for the sheep; such is the measure of His love.

He tends his flock like a shepherd: He gathers the lambs in his arms and carries them close to his heart.

ISAIAH 40:11 NIV

March 28

If you are physically well, praise God and learn not to complain about comparably minor irritations. If you do suffer from a physical infirmity, remember that the Lord is your strength and He will not only see you through this life, but He will give you a brand new body in the next life.

For it has been granted to you that for the sake of Christ you should not only believe in him but also suffer for his sake.

PHILIPPIANS 1:29 RSV

October 5

How many times do you and I fret and turn, looking for a little peace? God's peace can be in our hearts—right now. Ask for God's peace and see what a transformation will take place in your life.

Fear not, for I am with you; be not dismayed, for I am your God. I will strengthen you, yes, I will help you, I will uphold you with my righteous right hand.

ISAIAH 41:10 NKJV

March 29

Jesus Christ said: "I am the resurrection, and the life: he that believeth in me, though he were dead, yet shall he live: and whosoever liveth and believeth in me shall never die" (John 11:25-26). Our hope of immortality is based on Christ alone.

For me to live is Christ, and to die is gain.

PHILIPPIANS 1:21

October 4

When Job had lost everything he did not say, "The Lord gave and the devil has taken away," but "The Lord gave and the Lord has taken away; may the name of the Lord be praised." So when we are hurt, it is important to remember that God himself has allowed it for a purpose.

See, I have refined you, though not as silver;
I have tested you in the furnace of affliction.

ISAIAH 48:10 NIV

March 30

One of the most thrilling things about studying the Bible is to know that the infinite God has been pleased to share some of the secrets of His universe with His redeemed children. And what is God's will for us today? To know and to follow the will of God.

Teach me to do thy will.

PSALM 143:10

October 3

Comfort and prosperity have never enriched the world as adversity has done. Out of pain and problems have come the sweetest songs, the most poignant poems, the most gripping stories. Out of suffering and tears have come the greatest spirits and the most blessed lives.

For the Lord comforts his people and will have compassion on his afflicted ones.

ISAIAH 49:13 NIV

March 31

We are not filled (with the Spirit) once for all, like a bucket. Instead, we are to be filled constantly. The Christian is constantly to accept the direction and energy of the Spirit so he is always overflowing.

Do not get drunk on wine.... Instead, be filled with the Spirit.
EPHESIANS 5:18 NIV

October 2

We receive only one life during which we have many chances to come to know God. We are the biggest fools of all if we make the eternal mistake of rejecting the truth that God has communicated to us.

The fool hath said in his heart, there is no God.

PSALM 14:1

April 1

We may claim this promise from our Savior and Lord. He does go with us through our sufferings, and He awaits us as we emerge on the other side of the tunnel of testing—into the light of His glorious presence to live with Him forever!

Lo, I am with you alway, even unto the end of the world.

MATTHEW 28:20

October 1

After becoming a Christian, all of our life becomes a preparation for our journey to heaven. Are you going to heaven? Have you started packing yet?

For we know that if our earthly house of this tabernacle were dissolved, we have a building of God, an house not made with hands, eternal in the heavens.

2 CORINTHIANS 5:1

APRIL 2

There are thousands of people who do not give themselves to Jesus Christ, because they have conformed to the world. A true Christian does not conform himself to the worldly concepts of religion. Instead, he is to become a true "follower" of the Lord.

Be renewed in the spirit of your minds, and put on the new nature, created after the likeness of God in true righteousness and holiness.

EPHESIANS 4:23,24 RSV

September 30

Easter has been popularized and commercialized by merchants and the secular establishment. But the message of Easter is the central focus of Christianity. What does Easter mean to you? It means to me that Christ is risen!

"Don't be alarmed," he said. "You are looking for Jesus the Nazarene, who was crucified. He has risen! He is not here."

MARK 16:6 NIV

April 3

To resent and resist God's disciplining hand is to miss one of the greatest spiritual blessings we Christians can enjoy this side of heaven.

No discipline seems pleasant at the time, but painful. Later on, however, it produces a harvest of righteousness and peace for those who have been trained by it.

HEBREWS 12:11 NIV

September 29

If you trust the resurrected Christ as your Lord and Savior,
He will be with you when you die, and will give you life with
Him forever.

*God hath both raised up the Lord, and will also
raise us up by his own power.*

1 CORINTHIANS 6:14

April 4

God possesses infinite knowledge and an awareness which is uniquely His. At all times, even in the midst of any type of suffering, I can realize that He knows, loves, watches, understands, and more than that, He has a purpose.

Christ may dwell in your hearts through faith; [and] you, being rooted and grounded in love, may...know the love of Christ which surpasses knowledge.

EPHESIANS 3:17-19 RSV

September 28

Put Christ first in your life and then first in your marriage and you will have a bond between yourself, your mate, and the Lord that no one can break.

Therefore shall a man leave his father and his mother, and shall cleave unto his wife: and they shall be one flesh.

GENESIS 2:24

April 5

The only human hope for peace lies at the cross of Christ, where all men, whatever their nationality or race, can become a new brotherhood.

For he is our peace, who hath made both one, and hath broken down the middle wall of partition between us.

EPHESIANS 2:14

September 27

What would you do differently if you knew
Jesus was coming today?

The Lord is coming with fire, and his chariots are like a whirlwind; he
will bring down his anger with fury, and his rebuke with flames of fire.

ISAIAH 66:15 NIV

April 6

God is saying to the whole world, "I love you. I am willing to forgive your sins." God is saying to all those who are lonely today, "Behold, I am with you until the end of the age" (Matthew 28:20).

But now in Christ Jesus you who once were far off have been brought near in the blood of Christ.

EPHESIANS 2:13 RSV

September 26

The Bible says there are two kinds of wisdom in the world. First, there is wisdom that is given by God, a wisdom which views life in terms of eternity. The second is the wisdom of the world. Which kind of wisdom will you choose?

God hath chosen the foolish things of the world to confound the wise; and God hath chosen the weak things of the world to confound the things which are mighty.

1 CORINTHIANS 1:27

April 7

The man who has experienced the new birth is a member of God's household. His will is changed, his objectives for living are changed, his disposition is changed, his affections are changed, and he now has purpose and meaning in his life.

For we are his workmanship, created in Christ Jesus unto good works, which God hath before ordained that we should walk in them.

EPHESIANS 2:10

September 25

The hope we have in Christ is an absolute certainty. We can be sure that the place Christ is preparing for us will be ready when we arrive, because with Him nothing is left to chance. Everything He promised He will deliver.

Blessed is the man that trusteth in the Lord, and whose hope the Lord is.

JEREMIAH 17:7

April 8

The grace is God's: the faith is ours. God gave us the free will with which to choose. God gave us the capacity to believe and trust.

For by grace are ye saved through faith; and that not of yourselves: it is the gift of God: not of works, lest any man should boast.

EPHESIANS 2:8,9

September 24

It was love that enabled Jesus Christ to become poor
that we through His poverty might be rich.

*I have loved thee with an everlasting love: therefore with
lovingkindness have I drawn thee.*

JEREMIAH 31:3

Mar 1, 48   13ᵇ Ron Schubel
            April 9, 2015 died

God has provided us the power to resist the world and be separated from it, and it is ours to appropriate that power every hour of our lives. We are in the world, but the world is not to be in us.

I pray not that thou shouldest take them out of the world, but that thou shouldest keep them from the evil.

JOHN 17:15

September 23

No sin has been committed in the world today that can compare with the full cup of the universe's sin that brought Jesus to the cross. To you, sin may be a small thing; to God, it is a great and awful thing. It is the second largest thing in the world; only the love of God is greater.

For the preaching of the cross is to them that perish foolishness;
but unto us who are saved it is the power of God.

1 CORINTHIANS 1:18

April 10

Wherever you are at this moment, yield your life unconditionally to God, and He can still make it a thing of beauty and an honor to His name.

But God forbid that I should glory, save in the cross of our Lord Jesus Christ, by whom the world is crucified unto me, and I unto the world.

GALATIANS 6:14

September 22

The God of grace forgets our sins and wipes them completely from His memory forever! He places us in His sight as though we had never committed one sin. It is as if an accounting entry has been made in the books of heaven and the Divine Bookkeeper cancels our debt!

For I will forgive their iniquity, and I will remember their sin no more.
JEREMIAH 31:34

April 11

As a Christian you have the will-power to yield either to the flesh and live a fleshly, carnal life; or you have the power to yield to the Spirit, to live a Spirit-filled life. God meant the Christian life to be on the highest possible plane at all times, bearing the fruit of the Spirit.

The fruit of the Spirit is love, joy, peace, longsuffering, gentleness, goodness, faith, meekness, temperance.

GALATIANS 5:22,23

September 21

When a man comes in contact with God, He can never be the same again. God takes the weak and makes them strong, the vile and makes them clean, the worthless and makes them worthwhile, the sinful and makes them sinless.

I will give you one heart and a new spirit; I will take from you your hearts of stone and give you tender hearts of love for God.

EZEKIEL 11:19 TLB

April 12

Peace carries with it the idea of unity, completeness, rest, ease, and security. When you and I yield to worry, we deny our Guide the right to lead us in confidence and peace. Only the Holy Spirit can give us peace in the midst of the storms of restlessness and despair.

The fruit of the Spirit is...peace.
GALATIANS 5:22

September 20

The next time you have difficulty falling asleep at night (and even when you don't), read from the Psalms. Pick a quiet time in your house and a quiet place and let God soothe your troubled spirit to a point where you receive His rest and you place your trust and confidence in Him.

I will both lay me down in peace, and sleep: for thou, Lord, only makest me dwell in safety.

PSALM 4:8

April 13

UA StCld
320 255 6344 æ bills.

Living for Christ is a day-to-day walking with Him.
It is a continuous dependence upon the Spirit of God.
It is believing in His faithfulness. If we look to our own resources,
our own strength, or our own ability as Peter did when he
walked on the water, we will fail.

This I say then, Walk in the Spirit, and ye shall
not fulfil the lust of the flesh.
GALATIANS 5:16

September 19

The call of Christ is for rededication to Him—a call to follow Him, to pattern our lives after His. As John Wesley so wisely wrote: "Anything that cools my love for Christ is of the world."

Do not love the world or anything in the world. If anyone loves the world, the love of the Father is not in him.

1 JOHN 2:15 NIV

April 14

Without Jesus Christ in your heart, you can't have this love. You can't produce this love except with the power of the Holy Spirit. That's the reason you must receive Christ, and when you do, He gives you the power and the strength, through the Holy Spirit, to produce this love.

All the law is fulfilled in one word, even in this;
Thou shalt love thy neighbour as thyself.

GALATIANS 5:14

September 18

We owe God everything! We have been bought and paid for with a terrible price, the broken body and shed blood of God's Son.

I beseech you therefore, brethren, by the mercies of God, that ye present your bodies a living sacrifice, holy, acceptable unto God, which is your reasonable service.

ROMANS 12:1

April 15

In the midst of the pessimism, gloom, and frustration of the present hour there is one bright beacon light of hope—and that is the promise of Jesus Christ, "If I go and prepare a place for you, I will come again" (John 14:3).

We through the Spirit wait for the hope of righteousness by faith.

GALATIANS 5:5

September 17

Angels minister to us personally. We may not always be aware of the presence of angels. We can't always predict how they will appear. But angels have been said to be our neighbors. Often they may be our companions without our being aware of their presence.

Then Daniel said unto the king,...My God hath sent his angel, and hath shut the lions' mouths, that they have not hurt me.

DANIEL 6:21,22

April 16

Because God is responsible for our welfare, we are told to cast all our care upon Him, for He cares for us (I Peter 5:7). God says, "I'll take the burden—don't give it a thought—leave it to me." God is keenly aware that we are dependent upon Him for life's necessities.

For ye are all the children of God by faith in Christ Jesus.

GALATIANS 3:26

September 16

No words of men or angels can adequately describe the height and depth, the length and breadth of the glory to which the world awakened when Jesus came forth to life from the pall of death.

There was a violent earthquake, for an angel of the Lord came down from heaven and, going to the tomb, rolled back the stone and sat on it.

MATTHEW 28:2 NIV

April 17

Irenaeus said it well when he wrote, "The Word of God, Jesus Christ, on account of His great love for mankind, became what we are in order to make us what He is himself."

I am crucified with Christ: nevertheless I live: yet not I, but Christ liveth in me: and the life which I now live in the flesh I live by the faith of the Son of God, who loved me, and gave himself for me.

GALATIANS 2:20

September 15

The Scripture teaches that as Christians, our bodies may go to the grave but they are going to be raised on the great resurrection morning. Then will death be swallowed up in victory. As a result of the resurrection of Christ, death's sting is gone.

And God is going to raise our bodies from the dead by his power just as he raised up the Lord Jesus Christ.

1 CORINTHIANS 6:14 TLB

April 18

Evil is present to control and deceive us. We are not at peace with ourselves or with God. That is what the Cross of Christ is all about: to reconcile us to God and to give us a new nature.

Who gave himself for our sins, that he might deliver us from this present evil world, according to the will of God and our Father.

GALATIANS 1:4

September 14

One of the angels who was sitting outside the tomb proclaimed the greatest message the world has ever heard: "He is not here: for he is risen." Darkness and despair died; hope and anticipation were born in the hearts of men.

And the angel answered and said unto the women,
Fear not ye: for I know that ye seek Jesus, which was crucified.
He is not here: for he is risen, as he said.

MATTHEW 28:5,6

April 19

The Holy Spirit knows everything that we do—He watches us. "His eye is on the sparrow," and if God the Spirit is watching the sparrow, how much more is He watching us every moment.

The grace of the Lord Jesus Christ, and the love of God, and the communion of the Holy Ghost, be with you all.

2 CORINTHIANS 13:14

September 13

World problems are big, but God is bigger! If we will dare to take God into account, confess our sin, and rely unreservedly upon Him for wisdom, guidance, and strength, our world problems can yet be solved.

Break up your fallow ground, for it is the time to seek the Lord, that he may come and rain salvation upon you.

HOSEA 10:12 RSV

April 20

No one can be converted except with the consent of his own free will, because God does not override human choice. God helps a man when he takes the leap.

Except ye be converted, and become as little children, ye shall not enter into the kingdom of heaven.

MATTHEW 18:3

September 12

In our sufferings and tribulations Jesus himself must be our chief consideration. We must fix our eyes upon Him. He who suffered for us shows us how we are to bear our sufferings.

Though he were a Son, yet learned he obedience by the things which he suffered; and being made perfect, he became the author of salvation unto all them that obey him.

HEBREWS 5:8,9

April 21

It is not easy to be Christ's true follower. As someone has said, "Salvation is free but not cheap."

Everyone who wants to live a godly life in Christ Jesus will be persecuted.
2 TIMOTHY 3:12 NIV

September 11

True repentance is a turning from sin—a conscious, deliberate decision to leave sin behind—and a conscious turning to God with a commitment to follow His will for our lives. It is a change of direction, an alteration of attitudes, and a yielding of the will.

Turn ye even to me with all your heart...
with weeping, and with mourning.

JOEL 2:12

April 22

God sent His only Son into the world to die for our sins, so that we might be forgiven. This is a gift for us—God's gift of salvation. This gift is a permanent legacy for everyone who truly admits he has sinned. It is for everyone who reaches out and accepts God's gift by receiving Jesus Christ as his Lord and Savior.

Thanks be to God for his indescribable gift!

2 CORINTHIANS 9:15 NIV

September 10

In her book, *The Christian's Secret of a Happy Life,* Hannah Whitall Smith tells us: "What we need is to see that God's presence is a certain fact always, and that every act of our soul is done right before Him, and that a word spoken in prayer is really spoken to Him, as if our eyes could see Him and our hands could touch Him."

I will pour out my spirit upon all flesh.

JOEL 2:28

April 23

When was the last time you praised God in the midst of despair? Don't wait until you "feel like it" or you'll never do it. Do it, and then you'll feel like it!

We live on...sorrowful, yet always rejoicing; poor, yet making many rich; having nothing, and yet possessing everything.

2 CORINTHIANS 6:9,10 NIV

September 9

Upon the authority of God's Word, I declare that Christ is the answer to every baffling perplexity which plagues mankind. In Him is found the cure for care, a balm for bereavement, a healing for our hurts, and a sufficiency for our insufficiency.

The Lord will be the hope of his people,
and the strength of the children of Israel.

JOEL 3:16

April 24

Christ took our sins. He finished the work of redemption. I am not saved through any works or merit of my own. If we are believers in Jesus Christ, we have already come through the storm of judgment. It happened at the cross.

For he hath made him to be sin for us, who knew no sin; that we might be made the righteousness of God in him.

2 CORINTHIANS 5:21

September 8

When faced with the clouds of defeat we need to open our hearts and let Him in. Let Him take the clouds of sin out and transform you into a new creature.

Ask ye of the Lord rain in the time of the latter rain; so the Lord shall make bright clouds, and give them showers of rain, to every one grass in the field.

ZECHARIAH 10:1

April 25

Every person has been given a gift from God. You may be a farmer, or a laborer, or a doctor, or a professor, but you have been given a gift of the Holy Spirit. What is your gift? Each of us is to put his gift into action for God.

Stir up the gift of God which is in you.

2 TIMOTHY 1:6 NKJV

September 7

Death is robbed of much of its terror for the true believer, but we still need God's protection as we take that last journey.

So when this corruptible shall have put on incorruption, and this mortal shall have put on immortality, then shall be brought to pass the saying that is written, Death is swallowed up in victory.

1 CORINTHIANS 15:54

April 26

It is utterly impossible for me to change my disposition in my own strength. The new birth is something that must be done for me by another; and God has promised to do that which I cannot do for myself. And He will do it for you, too!

I will take away the stony heart...and I will give you an heart of flesh.
EZEKIEL 36:26

September 6

Only those who are poor in spirit and rich toward God shall be accounted worthy to enter heaven, because they come not in their own merit but in the righteousness of the Redeemer. Where is your treasure? In the bank? In the driveway? In the mirror? Or are you storing up your treasure in heaven?

For where your treasure is, there will your heart be also.

MATTHEW 6:21

April 27

Man—distressed, discouraged, unhappy, ruled by selfishness, quarrelsome, confused, depressed, miserable, taking alcohol and barbiturates, looking for escapisms—can come to Christ by faith and emerge a new man. This sounds incredible and yet it is precisely what the Bible teaches.

Old things are passed away; behold, all things are become new.
2 CORINTHIANS 5:17

September 5

It is our human nature to be proud, not meek. Only the Spirit of God can transform our lives through the new birth experience and then make us over again into the image of Christ, our example of what pleases God in the way of meekness.

Blessed are the meek: for they shall inherit the earth.
MATTHEW 5:5

April 28

In the last essay he wrote before he died, the great Christian apologist C. S. Lewis said, "We have no right to happiness; only an obligation to do our duty." It is only in our duty that happiness comes.

For our light affliction, which is but for a moment, worketh for us a far more exceeding and eternal weight of glory.

2 CORINTHIANS 4:17

September 4

Christ provided the possibility of purity by His death on the cross. The righteousness and the purity of God are imputed to all who confess their sins and receive Christ into their hearts.

Blessed are the pure in heart: for they shall see God.

April 29

Those who keep heaven in view remain serene and cheerful
in the darkest day.

*We are afflicted in every way, but not crushed; perplexed, but not driven
to despair; persecuted, but not forsaken; struck down, but not destroyed;
always carrying in the body the death of Jesus, so that the life of Jesus may
also be manifested in our bodies.*

2 CORINTHIANS 4:8-10 RSV

September 3

If we have peace with God and the peace of God,
we will become peacemakers. We will not only be at peace
with our neighbors, but we will be leading them to discover
the source of true peace in Christ.

Blessed are the peacemakers: for they shall be called the children of God.

MATTHEW 5:9

April 30

God has made some incredible promises to us. He has promised that we might have a relationship with Him through His Son. He has promised never to leave us.... Because of God's deposit on our lives, He is obligated to meet His promises. And so He has. And so He will.

For He who promised is faithful.
HEBREWS 10:23 NKJV

September 2

Think about it. Have you ever been persecuted for sharing your faith in Christ? Has your faith cost you anything? If not, perhaps you had better reexamine your faith.

Blessed are they which are persecuted for righteousness' sake: for theirs is the kingdom of heaven.

MATTHEW 5:10

May 1

When a loved one dies, it is natural for us to feel a sense of loss and even a deep loneliness. That will not vanish overnight. But even when we feel the pain of bereavement most intensely, we can also know the gracious and loving presence of Christ most closely.

Yea, though I walk through the valley of the shadow of death,
I will fear no evil: for thou art with me.

PSALM 23:4

September 1

Works are not ends in themselves, but they demonstrate God's love toward others so that they will know God loves them and so that they will desire to learn about God's provision for their greatest needs.

Faith without works is dead.

JAMES 2:20

Matt. 13:31-32

May 2

There are countless opportunities to comfort others, not only in the loss of a loved one, but also in the daily distress that so often creeps into our lives.

Blessed be the God and Father of our Lord Jesus Christ, the Father of mercies and God of all comfort, who comforts us in all our affliction, so that we may be able to comfort those who are in any affliction.

2 CORINTHIANS 1:3,4 RSV

August 31

Those who are persecuted for "righteousness' sake" are happy because they are identified with Christ. The enmity of the world is tangible proof that we are on the right side, that we are identified with our blessed Lord.

But I say to you, Love your enemies and pray for those who persecute you.

MATTHEW 5:44 RSV

May 3

Victory is yours. Claim it! This doesn't mean the Christian can never suffer defeat or experience low periods in life. But it does mean that the Savior goes with you no matter the problem.

Thanks be to God, who gives us the victory through our Lord Jesus Christ.

1 CORINTHIANS 15:57 RSV

August 30

Things have not really changed since that Bethlehem night two thousand years ago. God is still on the fringes of most of our lives. Are we in danger, in all of our busy activities, of excluding from our hearts and lives the One who made us?

And she brought forth her firstborn son, and wrapped him in swaddling clothes, and laid him in a manger; because there was no room for them in the inn.

LUKE 2:7

May 4

Once we have reached heaven, we will no longer be troubled or inhibited by physical or bodily limitations. The crippled, diseased, wasted bodies will be strong and beautiful and vigorous.

When the perishable has been clothed with the imperishable, and the mortal with immortality, then the saying that is written will come true: "Death has been swallowed up in victory."

1 CORINTHIANS 15:54 NIV

August 29

If a person gets his attitude toward money straight, it will help straighten out almost every other area of his life. The chief motive of the selfish, unregenerate person is "get." The chief motive of the dedicated Christian should be "give."

Take heed that you do not do your charitable deeds before men, to be seen by them.... But when you do a charitable deed, do not let your left hand know what your right hand is doing.

MATTHEW 6:1,3 NKJV

May 5

As we trust Christ to save us, we can be comforted in the knowledge that He waits on the other side to take our hand and welcome us into His (and our) dwelling place where the mansion He has prepared for us stands in readiness.

Listen, I will tell you a mystery! We will not all die, but we will all be changed.

1 Corinthians 15:51 NRSV

August 28

Living a holy life, leading others to Christ as we share our faith, doing good works in Christ's name, all of these things are materials that may be sent on ahead.

But lay up for yourselves treasures in heaven, where neither moth nor rust consumes and where thieves do not break in and steal.

MATTHEW 6:20 RSV

May 6

Death marks the beginning, not the end. It is a solemn, dramatic step in our journey to God.

The last enemy that shall be destroyed is death.

1 CORINTHIANS 15:26

August 27

We have the power to choose whom we will serve, but the alternative to choosing Christ brings certain destruction. Christ said that! The broad, wide, easy, popular way leads to death and destruction. Only the way of the Cross leads home.

You cannot serve both God and Money.

MATTHEW 6:24 NIV

May 7

Paul believed in Christ and committed his all to Christ. The result was that he knew Christ was able to keep him forever. Strong faith and living hope are the result of unconditional commitment to Jesus Christ.

For we know in part and we prophecy in part, but when perfection comes, the imperfect disappears.

1 CORINTHIANS 13:9,10 NIV

August 26

We were never meant to be crushed under the weight of care. We push the button of faith or pull the lever of trust, and our burden is discharged upon the shoulder of Him who said He would gladly bear it.

Therefore do not be anxious, saying, "What shall we eat?" or "What shall we drink?" or "What shall we wear?"

MATTHEW 6:31 RSV

May 8

We Christians should stand out like a sparkling diamond against a rough and dark background. We should be poised, cultured, courteous, gracious, but firm in the things we do or do not do. We should laugh and be radiant; but we should refuse to allow the world to pull us down to its level.

Moreover it is required in stewards, that a man be found faithful.

1 Corinthians 4:2

August 25

I don't believe any world leader will write the last chapter of history—God will write it. I believe...that there is a destiny for the human race far beyond anything we can dream. But it will be God's kingdom and will come in God's way.

But seek ye first the kingdom of God, and his righteousness;
and all these things shall be added unto you.

MATTHEW 6:33

May 9

John Wesley gave us a goal for goodness: "Do all the good you can, by all the means you can, in all the ways you can, in all the places you can, at all the times you can, to all the people you can, as long as ever you can."

I myself am convinced, my brothers, that you yourselves are full of goodness, complete in knowledge and competent to instruct one another.

ROMANS 15:14 NIV

August 24

Only God himself fully appreciates the influence of a Christian mother in the molding of character in her children. Every mother owes it to her children to accept Christ as her personal Savior, that she may be the influence for good in the lives of those whom Christ has graciously given to her.

They gave themselves first to the Lord and then to us in keeping with God's will.

2 CORINTHIANS 8:5 NIV

May 10

When faith is strong, troubles become trifles. There can be comfort in sorrow because in the midst of mourning, God gives a song.

Now the God of hope fill you with all joy and peace in believing, that ye may abound in hope, through the power of the Holy Ghost.

ROMANS 15:13

August 23

Good has a particular responsibility to his children;
oh, my anxious friend whose prayers have not been answered,
God invites you to the intimacy of spiritual sonship.

*Ask, and it will be given you; seek, and you will find; knock, and it will
be opened to you. For every one who asks receives, and he who seeks finds,
and to him who knocks it will be opened.*

MATTHEW 7:7 RSV

May 11

C. S. Lewis wrote, in *Christian Behavior:* "If you read history, you will find that the Christians who did most for the present world were those who thought most of the world to come. Aim at heaven and you will get earth thrown in. Aim at earth and you will get neither."

Through endurance and the encouragement of the Scriptures we might have hope.

ROMANS 15:4 NIV

August 22

God gives people the freedom to choose. If you sense a longing for God, a desire to change and be a new person, that's God speaking to your heart. And when you respond to Him, God will change you. Make a choice for Christ now.

No man can serve two masters: for either he will hate the one, and love the other; or else he will hold to the one, and despise the other.

MATTHEW 6:24

May 12

The death of the righteous is no accident. Do you think that the God whose watchful vigil notes the sparrow's fall and who knows the number of hairs on our heads would turn His back on one of His children in the hour of peril?

For whether we live, we live unto the Lord; and whether we die, we die unto the Lord: whether we live therefore, or die, we are the Lord's.

ROMANS 14:8

August 21

Life itself, every bit of health that we enjoy, every hour
of liberty and free enjoyment, the ability to see, to hear, to speak,
to think, and to imagine—all this comes from the hand of God.
We show our gratitude by giving back to Him a part of
that which He has given to us.

Freely ye have received, freely give.

MATTHEW 10:8

May 13

Christ must be vitally real to us if we are to remain faithful to Him in the hour of crisis. And who knows how near that hour may be? Things are happening fast! The need for a turning to God has never been more urgent.

Clothe yourselves with the Lord Jesus Christ, and do not think about how to gratify the desires of the sinful nature.

ROMANS 13:14 NIV

August 20

The invitation to discipleship is the most thrilling ever to come to mankind. Just imagine being a working partner with God in the redemption of the world!

If anyone serves me, let him follow me; and where I am, there will my servant also be. If anyone serves me, him will my father honor.

JOHN 12:26 NKJV

May 14

This is the ultimate proof that one is a disciple: if he follows the commands of his teacher. Jesus said that he that keeps God's commandments is the one who truly loves God.
Are you a disciple of the Lord Jesus?

So no one can become my disciple unless he first sits down and counts his blessings—and then renounces them all for me.

LUKE 14:33 TLB

August 19

To be sure, we must deplore wickedness and wrongdoing, but our commendable intolerance of sin too often develops into a deplorable intolerance of sinners. Jesus hates sin but loves the sinner.

The Son of Man came eating and drinking, and they say, "Here is a glutton and a drunkard, a friend of tax collectors and 'sinners.'" But wisdom is proved right by her actions.

MATTHEW 11:19 NIV

May 15

These bodies of ours are intended to be temples of the Spirit of God. We are to present them wholly to God as a "living sacrifice." Our dress, our posture, our actions should all be for the honor and glory of Christ.

Present your bodies a living sacrifice, holy, acceptable unto God, which is your reasonable service.

ROMANS 12:1

August 18

When we rest, we place our confidence in something outside of ourselves. Jesus gives us the confidence we need to escape the frustration and chaos of the world around us. Rest in Him and do not worry about what lies ahead. Jesus Christ has already taken care of tomorrow.

Come unto me...and I will give you rest.

MATTHEW 11:28

May 16

We do not understand the intricate pattern of the stars in their courses, but we know that He who created them does, and that just as surely as He guides them, He is charting a safe course for us.

O the depth of the riches both of the wisdom and knowledge of God! how unsearchable are his judgments, and his ways past finding out!

ROMANS 11:33

August 17

I must yield to Him...surrender to Him...give Him control of my life. Through that surrender I will find happiness!

Take my yoke upon you, and learn of me; for I am meek and lowly in heart: and ye shall find rest unto your souls.

MATTHEW 11:29

May 17

Christ is the answer to sadness and discouragement. He can put a spring in one's step and give one a thrill in his heart and a purpose in his mind. Optimism and cheerfulness are products of knowing Christ.

We know that in everything God works for good with those who love him, who are called according to his purpose.

ROMANS 8:28 RSV

August 16

The human mind cannot be a vacuum. It will be filled either with good or evil. It will be either carnal or Christlike. We can control the kind of thoughts that enter our minds. Some unknown wise man has suggested: "Give your mind to Christ that you may be guided by His wisdom."

Let this mind be in you, which was also in Christ Jesus.

PHILIPPIANS 2:5

May 18

That "the Spirit itself maketh intercession" indicates that it is actually God pleading, praying, and mourning through us. Thus we become co-laborers with God, actual partners with Him.

For we know not what we should pray for as we ought: but the Spirit itself maketh intercession for us with groanings which cannot be uttered.

ROMANS 8:26

August 15

What are the required courses in the university of life? You are going to have to face life; you are going to have to face death; you are going to have to face judgment. You can't really face any of them without Christ.

Take my yoke upon you, and learn from me.
MATTHEW 11:29 RSV

May 19

Affliction can be a means of refining and of purification. Many a life has come forth from the furnace of affliction more beautiful and more useful. Affliction may also be for our strengthening and Christian development. We learn through the trials we are called upon to bear.

I consider that our present sufferings are not worth comparing with the glory that will be revealed in us.

ROMANS 8:18 NIV

August 14

There is a sense in which the kingdom of God is already here in the living presence of Christ in the hearts of all true believers. There is also, however, the ultimate consummation of all things, which is called the kingdom of God.

The kingdom of heaven is like treasure hidden in a field, which a man found and covered up; then in his joy he goes and sells all that he has and buys that field.

MATTHEW 13:44 RSV

May 20

Because Christ rose from the dead, we know that sin and death and Satan have been decisively defeated. And because Christ rose from the dead, we know that there is life after death, and that if we belong to Him we need not fear death or hell.

The Spirit itself beareth witness with our spirit,
that we are the children of God.

ROMANS 8:16

August 13

Jesus' teaching was unique. He took God out of the theoretical realm and placed Him in the practical. He spoke with authority! He spoke with finality! He spoke as though He knew... and He did! Am I listening to Him—or am I a cynic as were so many of His countrymen?

"Where did this man get this wisdom and these mighty works? Is not this the carpenter's son?"

MATTHEW 13:54,55 RSV

May 21

Those who love Christ have that confidence in Him that raises them above fear. When I understand that Christ in His death gained a decisive victory over death and over sin, then I lose the fear of death.

For you did not receive a spirit that makes you a slave again to fear, but you received the Spirit of sonship. And by him we cry, "Abba, Father."

ROMANS 8:15 NIV

August 12

History has been changed time after time because of prayer. I tell you, history could be altered and changed again if people went to their knees in believing prayer.

And when he had sent the multitudes away, he went up into a mountain apart to pray: and when the evening was come, he was there alone.

MATTHEW 14:23

May 22

Self-analyzation can lead to depression. We need to keep our attention focused on Christ.

I do not understand my own actions. For I do not do what I want, but I do the very thing I hate.

ROMANS 7:15 RSV

August 11

Jesus Christ is who He said He is: God in human form.
And that is a crucial truth which undergirds the reality of our
salvation. Only the risen and ascended Son of God is worthy
of our worship and our service.

*Then they...came and worshipped him,
saying, Of a truth thou art the Son of God.*

MATTHEW 14:33

May 23

I f we in the church want a cause to fight, let's fight sin.

For the wages of sin is death; but the gift of God is eternal life through Jesus Christ our Lord.

ROMANS 6:23

August 10

The effective Christians of history have been men and women of great personal discipline. To be a true, effective disciple of Christ, we must seek to discipline our lives and endeavor to walk even as He walked.

Then said Jesus unto his disciples, If any man will come after me, let him deny himself, and take up his cross, and follow me.

MATTHEW 16:24

May 24

Instead of filling your mind with resentments, humbly give all over to God. Your conflicts will diminish and your inner tensions will often vanish. Then your life will begin to count for something.

Do you not know that to whom you present yourselves slaves to obey, you are that one's slaves whom you obey, whether of sin leading to death, or of obedience leading to righteousness?

ROMANS 6:16 NKJV

August 9

God has sent His Son, Jesus Christ, to the cross as a demonstration of His love and mercy. He asks us to come to that cross in a repentance of our sins and submission of our will to Him. He promises a peace treaty for all who will come by faith. Do you have Christ's peace in your life?

Great peace have they who love your law,
and nothing can make them stumble.

PSALM 119:165 NIV

May 25

Our human frame is often a rebellious and unruly servant. Only through rigid discipline are we able to master it into complete subjection to Christ.

Neither yield ye your members as instruments of unrighteousness unto sin: but yield yourselves unto God, as those that are alive from the dead, and your members as instruments of righteousness unto God.

x

ROMANS 6:13

August 8

Jesus Christ spoke frankly to His disciples and hid nothing from them. In unmistakable language, He told them that discipleship meant a life of self-denial and the bearing of a cross. He asked them to count the cost carefully.

For whosoever will save his life shall lose it:
and whosoever will lose his life for my sake shall find it.
MATTHEW 16:25

May 26

Nothing can harm us, including death, when we have trusted Christ as Savior, because Christ has conquered death—and so shall we.

Death no longer has mastery over him.

ROMANS 6:9 NIV

August 7

Christians are joint heirs with Jesus Christ through redemption, which is made theirs by faith in Him based on His death at Calvary.

For the Son of man shall come in the glory of his Father with his angels; and then he shall reward every man according to his works.

MATTHEW 16:27

May 27

Upon what is hope based? It is based upon the resurrection of Jesus Christ.

I am the resurrection, and the life: he that believeth in me, though he were dead, yet shall he live.

JOHN 11:25

August 6

The Scripture says that in the midst of persecution, confusion, wars, and rumors of wars, we are to comfort one another with a knowledge that Jesus Christ is coming back in triumph, glory, and majesty.

Wherefore comfort one another with these words.

1 Thessalonians 4:18

May 28

The cross, where Christ died in our place, is the only place to find forgiveness and have eternal life. Because Christ lives, I live also if I am in Him and He is in me.

Knowing this, that our old man is crucified with him, that the body of sin might be destroyed, that henceforth we should not serve sin.

ROMANS 6:6

August 5

The world's favorite verb is "get." The verb of the Christian is "give." Self-interest is basic in modern society. But in God's kingdom self-interest is not basic—selflessness is.

It is easier for a camel to go through the eye of a needle, than for a rich man to enter into the kingdom of God.

MATTHEW 19:24

May 29

The saved person is in God's safety zone, cleansed by the blood of Christ. The one who takes his stand at the Cross is saved forevermore. He can never come into condemnation.

Since we have now been justified by his blood, how much more shall we be saved from God's wrath through him!

ROMANS 5:9 NIV

August 4

One thing almost everyone who loves Jesus Christ agrees on— Jesus Christ is coming back. For the true believer in Jesus Christ, the future is assured. We wait the distant trumpet announcing the coming of Jesus Christ.

The disciples came to him privately, saying, "Tell us, when will this be, and what will be the sign of your coming and of the close of the age?"
MATTHEW 24:3 RSV

May 30

No matter what sin we have committed, no matter how black, dirty, shameful, or terrible it may be, God loves us. We may be at the very gate of hell itself, but God loves us with an everlasting love. Because of His love there is a way of salvation, a way back to God through Jesus Christ, His Son.

Greater love hath no man than this, that a man lay down his life for his friends.

JOHN 15:13

August 3

The return of Jesus Christ will be the most glorious and wonderful surprise of all for those who know Him and have committed their lives to Him. We should use every opportunity we have to tell others of our glorious Savior who wants all of us to live with Him forever.

Therefore you also must be ready; for the Son of man is coming at an hour you do not expect.

MATTHEW 24:44 RSV

May 31

The Bible teaches that "God is love" and that God loves you. To realize that is of paramount importance. Nothing else matters so much. And loving you, God has wonderful plans for your life.

God demonstrates His own love toward us, in that while we were still sinners, Christ died for us.

ROMANS 5:8 NKJV

August 2

There must be a practical outworking of our faith here in this present world, or it will never endure in the world to come. We need fewer words and more charitable works; less palaver and more pity; less repetition of creed and more compassion.

Verily I say unto you, Inasmuch as ye did it not to one of the least of these, ye did it not to me.

MATTHEW 25:45

June 1

Talking about the secret of Spirit-filled living, the great evangelist D. L. Moody said, "I believe firmly that the moment our hearts are emptied of pride and selfishness and ambition and everything that is contrary to God's law, the Holy Spirit will fill every corner of our hearts."

The love of God is shed abroad in our hearts by the Holy Ghost which is given unto us.
ROMANS 5:5

August 1

This is a glorious time to be alive. I have found that people everywhere will respond to the gospel of Jesus Christ if we present it simply, with compassion.

Go ye therefore, and teach all nations...teaching them to observe all things whatsoever I have commanded you: and, lo, I am with you alway, even unto the end of the world.

MATTHEW 28:19,20

June 2

We are not worthy to approach the holy throne of God except through Jesus Christ. The person who comes with confidence to the throne of grace has seen that his approach to God has been made possible because of Jesus Christ.

For through him we both have access by one Spirit unto the Father.

EPHESIANS 2:18

July 31

We can count on Christ's presence not only every day, but every moment of every day. Of the fact of His presence there can be no doubt, for His Word cannot fail. What we need is to cultivate the sense of His presence, every day, every hour, every moment.

I will be with you always, to the very end of the age.
MATTHEW 28:20 NIV

June 3

Charles Haddon Spurgeon shares, "The man who knows that his hope of glory will never fail him because of the great love of God, of which he has tasted, that man will hear music at midnight; the mountains and the hills will break forth before him into singing wherever he goes."

By whom also we have access by faith into this grace wherein we stand, and rejoice in hope of the glory of God.

ROMANS 5:2

July 30

Suffering is endurable if we do not have to bear it alone; and the more compassionate the Presence, the less acute the pain.

I will not leave you comfortless.

JOHN 14:18

June 4

There is no conflict in the heart where Christ abides, for His words, "Peace I leave with you" (John 14:27), have been proven in the test tubes of human experience over and over again, in the lives of those who have trusted His grace.

Therefore being justified by faith, we have peace with God through our Lord Jesus Christ.

ROMANS 5:1

July 29

Jesus was never too hurried to spend hours in prayer. He prayed before every difficult task confronting Him. He prayed with regularity—not a day began or closed on which He did not unfold His soul before His Father. Never stop praying no matter how dark and hopeless your case may seem.

And when he had sent them away, he departed into a mountain to pray.

MARK 6:46

June 5

The very presence of counterfeits proves the existence of the real. There would be no imitations without a genuine product. God's original design has always had imitators and counterfeits!

For they exchanged the truth of God for a lie, and worshiped and served the creature rather than the Creator, who is blessed forever. Amen.

ROMANS 1:25 NASB

July 28 2015 card to D.N

Jesus indicated that our problem is heart trouble. To have a spiritual awakening, the cross of Jesus Christ must be central in all teaching, preaching, and practice.

For it is from within, from the human heart, that evil intentions come: fornication, theft, murder, adultery, avarice, wickedness, deceit, licentiousness, envy, slander, pride, folly. All these evil things come from within, and they defile a person.

MARK 7:21-23 NRSV

June 6

Conscience is God's lamp within man's breast. Its very existence within us is a reflection of God in the soul of man. Our consciences can be purified as we allow God's Word, the Bible, to clean and enlighten them.

I myself always strive to have a conscience without offense toward God and men.

ACTS 24:16 NKJV

July 27

Surrender is the secret of victorious Christian living.
There needs to be confession of sin and a complete yielding of
every area of life, personality, and will to Jesus Christ—
plus faith that Christ will accept that commitment.

*Whosoever will save his life shall lose it; but whosoever shall lose his life
for my sake and the gospel's, the same shall save it.*

MARK 8:35

June 7

Many have been told to look for spiritual thrills, but the Bible says that "a man is justified by faith," and not by feeling. A man is saved by trusting in the finished work of Christ on the cross and not by bodily sensations and religious ecstasy.

Believe on the Lord Jesus Christ, and thou shalt be saved.

ACTS 16:31

July 26

God can use a sensitive Christian to be a rich blessing
in the life of one who knows pain and sorrow.

For the Son of man also came not to be served but to serve,
and to give his life as a ransom for many.

MARK 10:45 RSV

June 8

Christians can rejoice in tribulation because they have eternity's values in view. When the pressures are on, they look beyond their present predicament to the glories of heaven.

They returned...strengthening the souls of the disciples, exhorting them to continue in the faith, and saying that through many tribulations we must enter the kingdom of God.

ACTS 14:21,22 RSV

July 25

With God nothing is impossible. No task is too arduous, no problem is too difficult, no burden is too heavy for His love. The future is fully revealed to Him. We must learn the difficult lesson of praying as the sinless Son of God Himself prayed, "Not my will, but thine, be done."

Whatever things you ask when you pray, believe that you receive them, and you will have them.

MARK 11:24 NKJV

June 9

If you know Christ and have committed your life to Him, learn from Him and live a consistent life for Him. Do others see something of Christ—His love, His joy, His peace—in your life?

The disciples were filled with joy, and with the Holy Ghost.

ACTS 13:52

July 24

The precious hours of fellowship with His heavenly Father meant much more to our Savior than sleep, for the Bible says, "Jesus went out into the hills to pray, and spent the night praying to God" (Luke 6:12 NIV).

But Jesus often withdrew to lonely places and prayed.
LUKE 5:16 NIV

June 10

Thank God for the angelic forces that fight off the works of darkness. Angels never minister selfishly; they serve so that all glory may be given to God as believers are strengthened.

And Peter came to himself, and said, "Now I am sure that the Lord has sent his angel and rescued me from the hand of Herod."

ACTS 12:11 RSV

July 23

We Christians should dare to be different! Jesus' disciples influenced thousands to embrace the Christian faith because they out-thought, out-lived, and out-loved their neighbors.

If any man will come after me, let him deny himself, and take up his cross daily, and follow me.

LUKE 9:23

June 11

Our prayer must be for God's glory. If we are to have our prayers answered, we must give God the glory.

And whatsoever ye shall ask in my name, that will I do, that the Father may be glorified in the Son.

JOHN 14:13

July 22

We can be certain and worry-free about God's love, protection, and provision because He has never gone back on a single one of His promises. He never changes. Great is His faithfulness.

Consider the ravens: They do not sow or reap...yet God feeds them. And how much more valuable you are than birds!

LUKE 12:24 NIV

June 12

To be filled with the Spirit is to be controlled by the Spirit.
It is to be so yielded to Christ that our supreme desire
is to do His will.

*And when they had prayed, the place was shaken where they were
assembled together; and they were all filled with the Holy Ghost,
and they spake the word of God with boldness.*

ACTS 4:31

July 21

We ought to be men and women who are living disciplined lives, men and women who are following Christ in a Spirit-filled life. Having had your heart cleansed by the blood of Christ, having submitted and yielded every area of your life to Him, you can claim by faith to be filled with the Spirit.

Be filled with the Spirit.

EPHESIANS 5:18

June 13

The one and only way you can be converted is to believe on the Lord Jesus Christ as your own personal Lord and Savior. You can come "just as you are."

Neither is there salvation in any other: for there is none other name under heaven given among men, whereby we must be saved.

July 20

Christ calls us to follow Him, regardless of the cost, and He has never promised that our path will always be smooth. I have chosen Christ not because He takes away my pain but because He gives me strength to cope with that pain and in the long range to realize victory over it.

For which of you, intending to build a tower, does not sit down first and count the cost?

LUKE 14:28

June 14

Adrian baptized
at MFM church age 6

G od, through the refining fire of His Spirit, performs a
thousand miracles a day in the spiritual realm. His regenerating
power is ever at work in the world, taking the ashes of burned-out
lives and changing them to dynamic channels, dedicated to
winning the salvation of others!

This Jesus God raised up, and of that we all are witnesses.

ACTS 2:32 RSV

July 19   2015

Ron C died
at hosp
about 6:30 P

Not only does God love you, but the angels love you too. They are anxious for you to repent and turn to Christ for salvation before it is too late. They know the terrible dangers of hell that lie ahead. They want you to turn toward heaven, but they know that this is a decision that you and you alone will have to make.

There is joy before the angels of God over one sinner who repents.
LUKE 15:10 RSV

June 15

The early church had no church buildings, no Bibles,
no automobiles, no planes, no trains, no television, no radio.
Yet they turned their world "upside down" for Christ.
They instituted a spiritual revolution simply because
they were filled with the Spirit.

They were all filled with the Holy Spirit.

ACTS 2:4 RSV

July 18

Too often, things become our focus of worship. It is at that point that material goods become our masters rather than our servants. You must choose whom you will serve. Will it be God or money?

No one can serve two masters. Either he will hate the one and love the other, or he will be devoted to one and despise the other. You cannot serve both God and Money.

LUKE 16:13 NIV

June 16

Life is a glorious opportunity if it is used to condition us for eternity. If we fail in this, though we succeed in everything else, our life will have been a failure. One hundred years from this day you will be more alive than you are at this moment.

These are written, that ye might believe that Jesus is the Christ, the Son of God; and that believing ye might have life through his name.

JOHN 20:31

July 17

Even as the angels escorted Lazarus when he died,
so we can assume that they will escort us when by death
we are summoned into the presence of Christ.

*And it came to pass, that the beggar died, and was carried
by the angels into Abraham's bosom.*

LUKE 16:22

June 17

God created man with the capacity to love. Love is based upon one's right to choose to love. We cannot force others to love us. We can make them serve us or obey us. But true love is founded upon one's freedom to choose to respond.

We love him, because he first loved us.

1 JOHN 4:19

July 16

No matter what afflictions, pain, or distortions
we have in our earthly bodies, we will be given new bodies.
What a glorious promise of things to come!

*Jesus Christ...will transform our lowly body that it may be
conformed to His glorious body, according to the working by which
He is able even to subdue all things to Himself.*

PHILIPPIANS 3:20,21 NKJV

June 18

After you have given yourself completely to Christ in surrender to Him, remember that God has accepted what you have presented. You have come to Him; now He has received you. And He will in no wise cast you out!

I pray for them...for they are thine. And all mine are thine, and thine are mine; and I am glorified in them.

JOHN 17:9,10

July 15

If there are any tears shed in heaven, they will be over the fact that we prayed so little. Heaven is full of answers to prayer for which no one ever bothered to ask!

Be joyful in hope, patient in affliction, faithful in prayer.
ROMANS 12:12 NIV

June 19

Jesus dined with publicans and sinners, but He did not allow the social group to conform Him to its ways. Our social contacts should not only be pleasant, but also opportunities to share our faith with those who do not yet know Christ.

I have given them thy word; and the world has hated them, because they are not of the world, even as I am not of the world.

JOHN 17:14 RSV

July 14

The human race is rushing madly toward some sort of climax, and the Bible accurately predicts what the climax is! God's plan was inaugurated at the first coming of Jesus Christ. It will be completed at His second coming!

And then shall they see the Son of man coming in a cloud with power and great glory.

LUKE 21:27

June 20

We should refuse to support anything which does not meet with the approval of our Christian conscience. The Christian who refuses to compromise in matters of honesty, integrity, and morality is bearing an effective witness for Christ.

If ye were of the world, the world would love his own: but because ye are not of the world, but I have chosen you out of the world, therefore the world hateth you.

JOHN 15:19

July 13

That is the hope that is in the heart of every believer—
that our redemption is drawing nigh. Certainly we are two
thousand years nearer the coming again of the Lord Jesus Christ
than we were when He made those predictions.

*When these things begin to come to pass, then look up, and
lift up your heads; for your redemption draweth nigh.*

LUKE 21:28

June 21

Love is the real key to Christian unity. In the spirit of true humility, compassion, consideration, and unselfishness—which reflect the mind of the Lord Jesus—we are to approach our problems, our work, and even our differences.

These things I command you, that ye love one another.
JOHN 15:17

July 12

Just as surely as God implants the life cell in the tiny seed that produces the mighty oak, and as surely as He instills the heartbeat in the life of the tiny infant yet unborn, He implants His divine life in the hearts of men who earnestly seek Him through Christ.

Jesus answered him, "Truly, truly, I say to you, unless one is born anew, he cannot see the kingdom of God."

JOHN 3:3 RSV

June 22

Tears shed for self are tears of weakness, but tears of love shed for others are a sign of strength. Until I have learned the value of compassionately sharing others' sorrow, distress, and misfortune, I cannot know real happiness.

This is my commandment, That ye love one another, as I have loved you. Greater love hath no man than this, that a man lay down his life for his friends.

JOHN 15:12,13

July 11

Order is very important in most everything we do. By putting Jesus Christ and His will for your life first, everything else will fall into place. Try putting Christ first and watch how your life is turned around.

But seek ye first the kingdom of God, and his righteousness; and all these things shall be added unto you.

MATTHEW 6:33

June 23

If you read and reread Psalm 91, you will discover that in Him we have a permanent abode and residence, and that all of the comfort, security, and affection which the human heart craves is found in Him.

He that dwelleth in the secret place of the most High shall abide under the shadow of the Almighty.

PSALM 91:1

July 10

Revival is not more and not less than the presence of Christ in the heart, the home, the community, and the nation. Revival must begin with individuals. In the words of an old hymn, "Lord, send a revival, and let it begin with me."

Will you not revive us again?

Psalm 85:6 NIV

June 24

By faith accept the fact that you are indwelt by the Spirit of God. He is there to give you special power to work for Christ. He is there to give you strength in the moment of temptation.

And I will pray the Father, and he shall give you another Comforter, that he may abide with you for ever.

JOHN 14:16

July 9

Many men who have been used of God were great sinners and seemed unreachable. Don't give up on anyone. There is no man beyond the grace of God.

Christ Jesus came into the world to save sinners; of whom I am chief.

1 TIMOTHY 1:15

June 25

During Christ's ministry on earth He had no home, but His home in heaven will last forever. The early disciples and other Christian pilgrims suffered in many ways, but they were all eagerly anticipating the beauty and permanence of a never-ending home that lasts throughout eternity.

Foxes have holes and birds of the air have nests, but the Son of Man has no place to lay his head.

MATTHEW 8:20 NIV

July 8

"God is a Spirit—infinite, eternal and unchangeable." Those three words beautifully describe God. Men change, fashions change, conditions and circumstances change, but God never changes. Jesus Christ is the same yesterday, today and forever.

God is a Spirit; and they that worship him must worship him in spirit and in truth.

JOHN 4:24

June 26

Heaven is a permanent home. The venerable Bishop Ryle is reputed to have said: "Heaven is a prepared place for a prepared people, and they that enter shall find that they are neither unknown nor unexpected."

In my Father's house are many mansions: if it were not so, I would have told you. I go to prepare a place for you.

JOHN 14:2

July 7

Covet the will of God for your life more than anything in the world. You can have peace in your heart with little if you are in the will of God; but you can be miserable with much if you are out of His will.

Jesus said to them, "My food is to do the will of Him who sent Me, and to finish His work.

JOHN 4:34 NKJV

June 27

Abraham Lincoln once said, "I feel sorry for the man who can't feel the whip when it is laid on the other man's back."

By this shall all men know that ye are my disciples,
if ye have love one to another.

JOHN 13:35

July 6

No matter how sinful or unworthy we may feel today, God can use us. Throughout history God has chosen ordinary people and unworthy people and the least likely people. He can use us in our community, our town, our city, our country!

Many Samaritans from that city believed in him because of the woman's testimony, "He told me all that I ever did."

JOHN 4:39 RSV

June 28

We are made in the image of God. We are made to glorify God. We are made for God; and without Him there is an empty place in our life. That empty place can be filled by a simple surrender to Jesus Christ.

He that loveth his life shall lose it; and he that hateth his life in this world shall keep it unto life eternal.

JOHN 12:25

July 5

God will not force the new life upon us against our will.
We must be ready to receive Christ as Lord and Savior with all our
hearts. Then the miracle of the new birth takes place.

I tell you the truth, whoever hears my word and believes him
who sent me has eternal life and will not be condemned;
he has crossed over from death to life.

JOHN 5:24 NIV

June 29

One can have political freedom and still be a prisoner of sin, while one who is in a political prison and knows Christ can be more free than his jailers. Freedom in Christ is the ultimate freedom to be celebrated, not only on special days, but every day of the year.

If the Son therefore shall make you free, ye shall be free indeed.

JOHN 8:36

July 4

Why is Christianity so different from the religions of the world? It is because Christianity is not a religion. It is a relationship with a living God, Jesus Christ.

For just as the Father has life in himself, so he has granted the Son also to have life in himself; and he has given him authority to execute judgment, because he is the Son of Man.

JOHN 5:26,27 NRSV

June 30

Satan employs every device at his command to harass, tempt, thwart, and hurt the people of God. But the Christian is not left defenseless in this conflict. God provides power to give victory over Satan.

We wrestle not against flesh and blood, but against principalities, against powers, against the rulers of the darkness of this world, against spiritual wickedness in high places.

EPHESIANS 6:12

July 3

God puts no price tag on the Gift of gifts—salvation is free! Money can't buy it. Man's righteousness can't earn it. Social prestige can't help us acquire it. Morality can't purchase it. It is as Isaiah quoted: "Without money and without price."

I am the door: by me if any man enter in, he shall be saved.

JOHN 10:9

July 2

We are holding a light. We are to let it shine! Though it may seem but a twinkling candle in a world of blackness, it is our business to let it shine. Light dispels darkness, and it attracts people in darkness to it.

As long as I am in the world, I am the light of the world.
JOHN 9:5

July 1